Edited & Produced by Judi Paliungas
Upward Spiral Productions, Camarillo, CA
www.upwardspiralproductions.com

For information address: Life SOULutions.

Published by

Life SOULutions That Work, LLC
PO Box 630269 • Simi Valley, CA 93063
503-922-3460

www.MaryMorrissey.com

ISBN 978-0-9842225-0-6

Printed in China

For Karen Joyce

You truly are the CPO:
a Chief Possibility Officer for all who know you.
Your brilliance, guidance and generosity
inspired me to create the Miracle Minute.
May you know how much I love, respect, honor
and hold reverence for the being that is YOU.

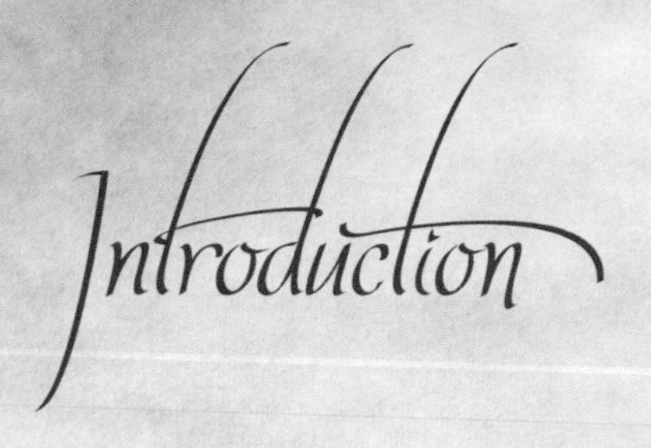

Introduction

Welcome to the *Miracle Minute*.

For over twenty-five years, my spiritual practice has included daily one-minute meditations.

Each day a new meditation, each day a new focus, each day a deeper relationship with Spirit.

Now, you are holding in your hands these one-minute meditations.

You can read this book front to back all at once, or one page every day, or open this book anywhere you want and enter into your own *Miracle Minute*.

With each *Miracle Minute* you are supported in focusing on what is really important, making choices for what is truly essential, and daily developing a deeper relationship with the Eternal.

May you enjoy and become more alive as you enter into your own adventure in the practice of the daily *Miracle Minute*.

—Mary Morrissey

A miracle is what happens when something so extraordinary occurs that coincidence is a foolish explanation.

—Mary Morrissey

Life by Design

Act As If

There is an old teaching story about a group of people in the Midwest who had been experiencing a drought that threatened all their crops. The minister called a town meeting so everyone could gather together to pray for rain.

Out of the entire community of hundreds of people, there was only one little boy, seven years old, who came to that prayer meeting carrying an umbrella.

You see, if we really believe it's going to rain, then we walk and we act differently, we come prepared—even in the midst of a drought.

So this day, whatever it is that you're visualizing, dreaming of, calling into form, remember that you are an image maker. You carry within you the power and the wonder and the glory; you bear witness to the image of God. We lay that power at the altar of limitation or we lay it at the altar of possibility every single day.

So today, whatever the umbrella symbology is for you, walk in this day as if what your are imaging is already happening. Notice that you begin to attract to yourself ideas, circumstances, and people, and how you begin to live with a license of a higher order of being.

Don't leave your home today without your umbrella!

I Can

Henry Ford said,

> *"If you think you can or you think you can't, you're right."*

So today let's expand the boundaries of the "I Can."

The I Can is way more important than the IQ. The I Can is the sense of possibility that dwells within us that is seeking—really pulling us—to expand so that the greatness and the glory and the wonder that indwells us might find the opportunity to express Itself right here, in this time. To allow us to give our gift to the family of this world.

So today, challenge every thought of "I can't," "I don't have," "I'm not enough," "I don't have what's required." Whatever those thoughts are, just challenge them and say, "What if I could?" Because, the "I" that indwells me is greater than anything I've ever done, anything I've ever had and anything I've ever learned—that "I" is God.

What if I can? Find out, you're going to be right.

The Marrow of Life

Henry David Thoreau made a decision to go to Walden Pond to simplify his life and to, as he said, "suck the marrow of life." Then he wrote this:

> *"I learned this at least by my experiment: that if one advances confidently in the direction of their dreams, and endeavors to live the life which they have imagined, they will meet with a success unexpected in common hours. They will put some things behind, will pass an invisible boundary; new, universal, and more liberal laws will begin to establish themselves around and within them; or old laws be expanded and interpreted in their favor in a more liberal sense, and he will live with the license of a higher order of being."*

IF one is willing to confidently move in the direction of their dreams and endeavor to live the life which one has imagined.

To do this, we have to know what our dreams are and imagine those dreams as a living reality that we can begin to inhabit, incorporate, and incarnate right where we are.

So perhaps the greatest work we'll do this day is let ourselves suck the marrow of life and do some dreaming and imagining.

Intention

I once heard someone say, "Where you place your attention, you are placing your intention." In fact, the only way the Universe knows what we are truly desiring is by where we are placing our attention; because the Universe gives us the power of focus and the power of free will.

Where we focus our attention with our free will builds an energy field that by the Law of Attraction attracts unto us the molecular structure of those thoughts. Where we're placing our attention today—and every day—creates a pattern of experience, a pattern of possibility and a pattern of attraction.

That is why it is so powerful for us to remember to take our minds off of our problems and put them on God. Take our minds off of what's missing or what seems wrong and put our minds on possibility and opportunity. To look for the good and to appreciate, because in that field, only more of the good can be made manifest in our lives.

So today, we take our attention and we put it on God and we give thanks for this day, another day of living.

God's Prosperity Plan

What if you could know God's plan for you? What if you could really know God's plan for you?

In the Bible, in Jeremiah the prophet writes,

> *"I know the plans I have for you…"*

says God. Says the God of the Universe, the God of your own being, the God who made you.

> *"Hear the plans I have for you, plans for your happiness, plans for your fulfillment, plans for your full creativity, plans for everything that is uplifting and life giving."*

That's God's plan for us. Anything less than that is outside of God's will. So when we're struggling, when we're too busy, when we're over-tired, when we're out of sorts; we're outside of God's will.

So let us do one thing today and take a deep, deep breath of life. And let's just come back into God's will and listen to our joy. Tune into love. See how we can make a difference for good.

Today God says to you and me, "The plans I have for you are plans for happiness and fulfillment."

The Cost of Life

In Concord, Massachusetts, Henry David Thoreau was a handyman for Ralph Waldo Emerson and his family. The author Nathaniel Hawthorne would often come and visit. Louisa May Alcott and her father, and many others would gather in this home—Sunday evenings in particular—and they would sit together, talk and share deep thoughts and their considerations of the week.

It was Thoreau who reminds us that what we do each day is what we are trading our lives for. He says:

> *"I went to the woods because I wished to live deliberately. To confront only the essential facts of life and see if I could not learn what the essential had to teach and not when I came to die, discover that I had not lived. I learned that the cost of a thing is the amount of what I will call life which is required to be exchanged for it."*

Is what we are spending our time doing worth our life cost?

Let us realize that today what we do and what we think about, what we feel is the cost of life. We are spending our life for what we do, so let us choose only what is really essential.

Metamorphosis

I once heard it said,

> *"A caterpillar can fly, but not as a caterpillar."*

A caterpillar has to be willing to go through a metamorphosis. There are imaginal cells in the caterpillar that begin to activate that transformation.

Now at first, the caterpillar's memory of what the caterpillar is and its immune system fights those imaginal cells. But ultimately, because they are of a higher power, those imaginal cells take over and the caterpillar submits to the transformation that brings forth the butterfly.

So my friend, what is the butterfly of you seeking to emerge this day? What is that butterfly? You can fly. You can do whatever it is that is in your heart, burning to come forth—but not with the caterpillar image you've held of yourself.

So what is the butterfly image of you? Know this, that image is God's dream for the next stage of your life. Get in touch with that image—it's you!

Think Big

You have Life energy in you. Living—with all its attributes—is something that doesn't just happen to touch a fortunate few.

It is simply seeking your awareness and your direction through intelligent use of the power of your thought for the good you desire to experience and to give.

Although our thoughts are invisible to physical sight they are an actual force or substance, as real as electricity, light, heat, water, or even stone.

According to Spirtual Law, the Life that patterns this invisible substance into the outward form of your inward thinking, will manifest through you in a particular way that that is uniquely suited to what you focus upon.

We are surrounded by a vast ocean of thought stuff. Our thoughts pass like currents of electricity or tiny streaks of light. It's just as easy for us to think around the globe, as it is to think across the room. Pay attention to that.

It takes no more energy to dream a big dream, than it does to think puny ideas. Think thoughts the size of the success you would like to have. This subtle element is fast and powerful.

So let your imagination run free today in the realm of your greatest dreams. Think thoughts that feel good to you. Today will never happen again. Take the reins of your thinking and have a great day!

Your Great Purpose

I wanted to share with you this day a reading from the Indian saint, guru and teacher Patanjali. He says:

> *"It is really quite exciting when we pay attention to what living on purpose can mean. When you are inspired by some great purpose, some extraordinary project, all of your thoughts break their bounds. Your mind transcends limitations, your consciousness expands in every direction and you find yourself in a new, great, and wonderful world. Dormant forces, faculties, and talents become alive and you discover yourself to be a greater person by far than you ever dreamed yourself to be."*

What is a great purpose? What is an extraordinary project? Something that matters to you. Something that deeply and profoundly matters to you.

So my friend, today, spend some time getting clear about what matters most to you. Ask the Holy Spirit to reveal to you an extraordinary project—a deep purpose for you to dedicate yourself to—and break the bounds of limitation.

Intelligent Design

What is it you'd like to experience? Take a breath and ask yourself: "What do I really want? Do I want prosperity? Do I want abundance? Do I want freedom from lack and limitation?"

Give yourself some room, breathe into it.

Remember, no one is repeatable, just as rare and unique as your own thumbprint is, the Universe knew what it was doing when it made you. You are made of the stuff of the Universe, the Spirit of the Universe, Creativity Itself.

Allow that Creativity to move up and rise up in your awareness. What would it be like to live that life you truly desire?

Now, as best as you can, step into that life imaginally. Walk around as the person who is living the life you imagine.

Like building a house step-by-step, we begin with drawings and we move forward systematically until completion. You will design your life either by default or by intelligent design; a design that you choose, and then pattern your life by.

Spend some time today designing your mental blueprint of your ideal life. You are worthy of your biggest dream!

Anything We're Willing to Become

There is a spiritual law that says you can have anything you are willing to become. We do live in a world that operates by the Law of Attraction and we have a magnetic radius to the energy that we primarily hold.

So, if we're wanting to bring something into our lives or experience a new result, the place to begin is within ourselves. It's an inside out Universe. We can have anything we're willing to become.

What would you like to bring in your life? Let's each think of that right now, and then ask, "Am I willing to become that? If not now, when?"

So today, walk in the world radiating the very thing you want to bring in your life. If you want more friendship, radiate friendship. If you want more love and some close companionship, then be loving to every person you meet in the most appropriate way. But, be that. Be the very thing you'd like to bring into your life.

Each one of us can truly and really have anything we're willing to become.

A Successful Day

Eleanor Roosevelt was once asked, "What are the three measures of a successful day?" She said that at the end of the day she measures her day according to these measurements of success:

1. *Was she honest with herself and others?*
2. *Did she try her very best that day?*
3. *Was this a day in which she had increased her ability to love others?*

Isn't that great! What great measurements for the success of a day at a time of a life lived well.

1. *Am I honest today with myself and others? Can I increase, deepen, and expand that honesty?*
2. *Is this a day where I'm bringing all I have to the table of the activity of my life?*
3. *Is this a day where I can increase (of course I can if I focus on it) my ability to both give and receive love?*

A successful life is lived one day at a time.

The Advancing Life

The Next Step

The shepherd boy who was the psalmist who would be King David said once, "The Lord is like a lamp unto my feet, casting a light upon my path."

The law, the light, the Presence, the Power that is God is like a lamp unto my feet directing my next step.

When I take that step, then the next step is shown. I'm not shown a mile down the road. I'm not shown a year down the road. I am shown just one day at a time the next step that is mine to take.

How powerfully comforting it can be for each one of us to know that we don't have to figure it all out. In fact, we can't; but the Universe does—and is—revealing to each one of us in a perfected way, uniquely to us, our own destiny. The greatest fulfillment we will ever find is in taking that step that is ours to take today.

So for a moment, let's just pause and ask, "What is my step to take today? What is mine to do today? What is mine to be grateful for today?

Let's bring ourselves fully to this day. "The Lord is a lamp unto my feet, casting a light upon my path"—and that lamp is shining brightly for you right now.

Knowing Ourselves

It was the thirteenth-century poet, Rumi, who said,

> *"It's as if the king has sent you into a far and distant land with one specific task to accomplish. You can accomplish a hundred other things but if you fail to accomplish the one thing for which you have been sent, it will be as if you have done nothing."*

As if you have done *nothing*.

A king, the G-O-D, the Grand Overall Designer of the Universe has sent us into a far and distant land—planet Earth, human birth, this grand opportunity called our lifetime—with one specific task to accomplish, which is the realization and the revealing of who we truly are, the authentic Self, the real Self, the son, the daughter of God that each one of us is.

We could accomplish a hundred other things. We could amass great wealth. We could demonstrate great authorities and powers, but if we miss knowing who we truly are and sharing our own unique gift with the world, it will be as if we have done nothing.

So this day, amid all the doing, pause right now, take a deep breath and say, "May I know myself better this day. May I give of myself better this day. May I receive the Self that I truly am with every thought, with every breath, with every action, sharing it with my world. I could accomplish a hundred other things but without this, it is as if I have done nothing."

Solutions

It was Albert Einstein who said,

> *"The significant problems we face cannot be solved at the level of thinking that created them."*

Thinking in the problem and thinking about the problem is thinking in the same vibration as the problem. Henry Kaiser said, "Problems are opportunities dressed in work clothes." So, whatever our problems are, they cannot be solved at the level of thinking of the problem.

So how do we raise our thinking to a place where solutions exist?

One clue, when you hear yourself thinking how big the problem is, you say to that problem, "There's an energy, a Power in this Universe that is way bigger than you."

When you say to yourself, "It can't be handled" or "I don't know what to do," instead say, "What if I did know what to do? What if the answer was already accessible to me because I'm already right at the center of the mind of God?"

For a moment today, find yourself thinking in an expanded way. Open up and say to yourself, "Right where I am, the wisdom of the Universe is. Right where I am, answers to every question are accessible because right where I am, God is."

The problems I'm facing cannot be solved at the level of thinking that creates them but there is another level of thinking available. It's available right where I am because right where I am, God is.

An Examined Life

I've been cleaning out my garage. As I'm working, I come upon things to sort out, things to let go of, things to keep and things that I wonder how I ever collected.

You know cleaning out our lives is very much the same way. We need to take the time to really take an honest look. It was Henry David Thoreau who said,

"An unexamined life is not worth living."

So as we go through our own mental closets and our own emotional closets, and notice some of the things we have held on to—it's time now to let them go.

Let today be a day of letting go of the things it is time to let go of, re-sorting some of the things you want to make important in your life, taking a look at priorities and just remembering, it isn't the things we do, it's energy we do them from. Mother Teresa said, "It is not that we do great things, but we do the things we do with great love."

Today, may all we do and set as our priorities come from great love.

Intention

In ancient Greece, the discus throwers were judged not just on how far they threw the discus, but on how they intended to throw the discus.

This is how the judging went: When the participant came forward in the early Olympics, he would hold up the discus and offer the discus to God, offer his throw to God and offer the avid intent for that particular throw to be an offering.

I just loved that story when I heard it, because I realized when we go through our day, we don't just make movements, we don't just speak words; there is an intention with everything we do. If we, right now, just make a decision; we're holding up our life for the whole rest of the day as an offering unto God, as an offering unto life, as an offering unto love.

So, as we hold this day, we're holding up ourselves and we're holding up everything we're doing as an offering.

A Million Dollar Idea

Earl Nightingale tells a story about a businessman who hired a very expensive business coach, Ivie Lee, to come and take a look at his business and show him how he could amplify his effectiveness and his income in a quantum way.

Lee looked at the way this other businessman was doing his work. He looked at the businessman's work style, his work, his methods, his effectiveness and then his recommendation was this:

> *"Every day before you leave your work, make a list. The next day when you come to work, pick only what is most important on that list. Do that. Either get it completely accomplished or do every single thing you can in regard to what's most important and then move on to the second most important item on the list."*

The businessman looked at Ivie Lee and said, "You mean for this I'm supposed to pay you all this money, just for that one idea?" Lee said, "Well how about this, do it completely for thirty days, then you pay me what you think it's worth." Thirty days later Ivie Lee got a check from the businessman for $30,000, which in today's world is about $150,000. He said, "This idea, when put into practice, revolutionized my work and my life."

So my friends, why don't we make a list at the end of each day of what's most important in our lives, and the following day make sure what is most important is receiving most of our energy. Let's do that for the next thirty days and decide by next month if in fact this was not a million dollar idea to each one of us as well.

Clearing Out the Weeds

In the Springtime, many people clear out their gardens and plant new flowers while investing energy in the natural cycle we call Springtime.

An idea we might have, each one of us, is do that same thing both emotionally and mentally. We don't plant new flowers in a garden that is filled with all kinds of weeds. We take a little time and we clear out the weeds.

So, today as we're going through our day, let's picture the mind field of our own thoughts as a garden that needs to be cleared out and prepare the soil for what we would really like to be harvesting. What would be the kind of seed you would plant this day?

You know, the great thing about it is all we have to do is ask God, and God will open up a way for us to find a way to clear the garden and plant that seed. Amazing things will start to happen—not just the thoughts we're thinking, but amazing things we can't even imagine!

Find Your Support

I heard Dr. John DeMartini say one time,

> *"Support plus challenge equals the best formula for growth."*

Right now, consider your life and where the challenge is and what the support for that challenge is. Know that life takes care of the challenge, but it is up to you to take care of the support. That doesn't mean that life isn't providing the support, but it means it is up to us to look for and appreciate and then draw to us the kind of support that will help us not only meet, but surmount that challenge. That is how we grow.

Sometimes support is found by amplifying the way we give support. Sometimes support is found by the way we appreciate the support that is in our environment right now. Sometimes support is found by choosing to play a piece of music that is inspiring, or sitting down for five minutes and reading something that inspires and uplifts us, or found by pausing for a moment to look at nature and appreciating the wonder and glory of what is all around us right now.

Support plus challenge equals the best formula for growth and all of life is inviting you and me this day… grow, grow, grow.

Clear the Clutter

Today is a day to get rid of one piece of clutter from your life. We clutter our lives with things we've acquired, with mental activity, with pressing plans, with our "to do" lists.

What could you just simply remove? Clear out one drawer in your kitchen or one drawer somewhere in your house. Move one box and empty it and get rid of the things in it.

Today, let one piece of clutter leave your life and notice the freedom of the energy as it begins to move through you. Notice the feeling of lightness as you release some of the block between it and you.

The God of our being is right where we are. We live in the material world. We distance ourselves from God with clutter. There is something very powerful in clearing a bit of clutter because what it opens up to us is the flow of the Power that is right where we are.

So today, whether it is a mental clutter, an emotional clutter, or a physical clutter; let us each make a commitment and say, "Today I release clutter and find God." Try it—just one little piece of clutter. Clear it out and notice what happens!

The Right Track

I was reading through some Will Rogers quotes. He said something that I had heard before, but at the time I didn't know it was actually Will Rogers who had said it. This particular quote always rings the tone of "you know what, this is really true." He said,

> *"Even if you're on the right track, you'll get run over if you just sit there."*

Even if you're on the right track, you'll get run over if you just sit there.

So today, what one step would you take to move yourself forward on the track you know you're destined to be on? Your right track.

What is the right track for you? What is one step you can take in the right direction? True north never changes and you have an inner compass that is aligned with your true north.

Keep in mind, even if we're on the right track and we just sit there— we'll go nowhere. But today we're not going to do that. Instead we're going to take that one step that moves us forward in the right direction.

Enthusiasm

It was Norman Vincent Peale who spoke so eloquently about enthusiasm. This is what he said:

> *"Enthusiasm is that mysterious something that turns an average person into an outstanding individual. It lifts us from fatigue to energy. It pulls us from mediocrity to excellence. It turns on a bright light in our life until our face glows and our eyes sparkle. It's a joyful, spiritual magnet that draws the best in life to us. The joyful fountain that bubbles and causes people to come to our side and share their joy. And out of this fountain, there leaps a self-confidence that shouts to the world with God, I can. It's possible. Enthusiasm is a long sought-after fountain of youth. When old men and women stop to drink of its elixir, they suddenly dream new dreams and mysterious energy surges through the body that moments before was fatigued, weary, and old."*

Now he knew something about this. He lived well into his '90s making huge differences for our world. He's saying enthusiasm is the long sought-after fountain of youth. Drink from this fountain of enthusiasm and you will experience a miracle. Discouragement will fade. Enthusiasm opens your heart to this moment right now where it is beckoning you into a whole new life's dream.

So today we can choose to be enthusiastic. Choose to drink from that fountain of youth that springs right from the center of our own being.

Sing a Song

There was an article in the Los Angeles Times about the power of singing. Not singing in public, and not singing with others, but by ourselves—in the car, in the shower, when we're alone or with someone we trust that isn't judging our voice.

The article goes on to say that it makes intuitive sense that singing is psychologically good. It can elevate one's mood, and provides an outlet for sadness.

But a growing body of science shows that not only is singing mentally healthy, it's also physically good for you. It improves the body's immune response. It reduces the use of prescription drugs, doctor visits, and emergency room–care visits. The conscious breathing from the diaphragm involved in singing can itself, reduce stress.

The old adage, "Don't die with your song in you," is true. Don't let this day end without having sung a little bit. It opens the door to some fun, some healing, and a whole new perspective.

Awareness

Seeing the Soul

What was so powerful about the ministry of Yeshua ben Joseph, who became Jesus, the Christ, was how people felt in the way in which he saw them. He saw them in their wholeness. He saw them in their natural beauty. He saw them in their wonder.

One of the greatest gifts we can bring to every person we meet today is to look at them beyond the personality level. We don't just see them as their history or what they look like at a physical level. But, let's bring the practice—and perhaps it might be the highest practice of our day—to practice seeing essence. Practice seeing the real being, the real person. Practice seeing the great soul in the amazing disguise of the human flesh that we see with each and every person we meet this day.

In that type of seeing, we are actually helping anchor heaven on Earth because we're helping—by this amplified seeing—someone in front of us, behind us, beside us, around us, and also that person inside of us. Recognize, re-cognize, that right where we are, God is.

Let's practice seeing God in everyone we meet this day.

Mindful Appreciation

In Plum Village, France, there lives a Vietnamese Buddhist monk, Thich Nhat Hanh, who has done so much to help increase our awareness of how we can be in the present and open to the miracle that is always presenting itself in each and every moment. He encourages us to do something called "mindfulness breathing."

I have heard that they ring a bell in Plum Village usually three to five times a day. No one ever knows exactly when the bell is going to ring. When the bell is rung, they pause, and they take a deep breath of mindful appreciation and gratitude for this precious human birth. I love that ideal.

Over the years, I've used other cues to help me remember to take a mindfulness breath. To be mindful of the precious gift of life.

One of those "bells" for me over the years has become door handles. Whenever I touch a door handle—whether it's to a room or to a car—anything that is a handle; it reminds me to pause and take even just one breath and say "Thank you God for this life."

So, whatever might be the bell of remembering for you, pick a bell today whether it is door handles or the sound of the bell or the phone ringing; something that will remind you to say, "Thank you God for this precious life."

Begin to practice that today and you will find more miracles than you can imagine.

Sureties

It is said that St. Patrick began each day with this particular prayer:

> *"Today I take for my sureties…"*

Now before I go on, let's pause for a moment and each one of us ask ourselves, "What are we absolutely sure about today?"

The truth is we can't even really be sure about the next breath, but we can be sure that no matter how the next breath occurs, there is a presence and there is a power that is with us in the breath and beyond the breath.

That is what St. Patrick stood in and stood from. There is miracle after miracle of how that way of living is accounted in his life.

You and I are invited to live from that miracle as well. It comes from knowing,

> *"Today I take for my sureties,*
> *God before me. God behind me.*
> *God above me. God below me.*
> *God all around me.*
> *God within me. God."*

Experiencing Miracles

In *A Course in Miracles* it says that if you and I are not experiencing miracles on a daily basis, it is we who are out of alignment with God.

It isn't that we have to call God in to make miracles happen. It is that we have to bring our attention to the presence of God before miracles become natural.

What are miracles but the parting of the waters of our problems? What are miracles except the healing of our blindness so that we can see more fully? What are miracles but the healing of parts of us that are paralyzed so that we can really take the steps that are ours to take? What are miracles but a shift in perception that removes a block in our minds to the love of God right where we are.

Miracles are natural to you and me because of our nature. Our nature is to be one with God. So if we are not experiencing miracles, it is we who need to move.

So today we put our attention on God and watch everything begin to move into the alignment with what is natural, and that is always a miracle.

Anchoring Peace

Mahatma Gandhi said,

> *"My religion is truth. My practice is non-cooperation with evil."*

Gandhi came from a practice which increased soul force or "Ahimsa." "Satyagraha" is what he called the practice of non-violence which he said was more powerful than any force or power that came from the world.

So you and I have the opportunity to anchor peace in our world right where we are. We can bring that about today. We can bring about the peace that we long for—for our world, for our families, for ourselves—by taking on his practice.

My religion is truth. Religion means to bind. So let us bind ourselves to the truth this day and notice if we cannot stay absolutely, pristinely adhered to whatever is true in the moment. Speak from that. Know that.

As we do that, simply choose not to cooperate with anything less than that, and from there, we live our lives in love and offer that to the world.

Sons and Daughters of God

In the Bible there's a wonderful scripture that says,

> *"Behold what manner of love is this, that you and I should be called sons and daughters of God."*

Behold, which means to pause for a moment and reflect and let yourself feel. What manner of love is this that you or I should be called a son or a daughter of God?

If you and I are a son or a daughter of God, that means we are in a relationship and we can experience a companionship, a friendship, a mentorship, a guide, a comfort and a provision.

So today, keep this in the forefront of your mind and your heart. Behold what manner of love is this that I, with everything that I've ever done or not done, with every mistake I've ever made, with every good thing I've ever done, with all of me that makes me, me—every part of it, in a way I can't even begin to understand, is part of a tapestry that is God's plan for my life.

Behold what manner of love is this that I am right now a son, a daughter of God and I can have this relationship more fully today than ever before in my life if I choose.

God's Fingerprint

When you think back over your life, there have been many moments when you have absolutely experienced mastery. When you've known that there is a part of the genius of the universe at work in you.

Think back to a moment when it might have been, perhaps when you were standing on a mountaintop after a long climb, and you looked out over the vast beauty of nature, and you felt your connection to that which is immense.

It's, in a way, a perfection that is beyond your own understanding. You felt that quickening inside yourself of awe and appreciation.

It might have been a moment when you did something that you know made a difference for good and you felt that feeling of "ahh." It might have been a moment when you had some kind of achievement, or earned a degree, or had a baby. For a moment in time, all of life comes together.

Do you know that those moments are really the fingerprint of God showing you and me how life is supposed to be? Today is a day to pay attention. God's fingerprint is all over your life. Pay attention to the mastery, to the miracle, to the wonder that is already showing up in your life this day. The way to see that is through appreciation.

So we enter this day now, with a new appreciation for the Master's fingerprint all over our life.

Where I Am, God Is

I heard a story that really moved me about one of the students at Virginia Tech, who—two days before the mass shooting there—emailed his mother and said, "I'm having a crisis of faith and I don't know if I even believe in God, but don't worry mom, I'm sure I'll get through this."

Two days later, in a classroom where there is a gunman systematically aiming a gun at each student and murdering them, this young boy is hiding under a desk and begins to pray, "God, make me invisible, God, make me invisible." That gunman walked through that room and never saw that boy—the one and only student who survived that classroom.

How is it that Spirit works in such a way that first we feel the longing, and the answer is provided when we are the person who can allow ourselves to be the place where the power of God can work?

May today be a day we deepen our faith and broaden our experience and awareness that right where I am, God is.

Illumination

I bet sometime today you actually reached over and turned on a light switch and you weren't really amazed that there was illumination that came into your room.

How come? Because you knew that the power was there and all that was required was you reach over and turn on the switch.

Well, you know that switch is within our hearts, and within our minds. The power to bring about, to heal, to transform, to change whatever we would is right where we are.

But sometimes, it's as if we stand in front of that light switch and plead and beg for the light switch to work. We have no idea that we have to play our part as well. The electric light switch "works" when it is in harmony with the law of electricity. Our lives "work" when we are in harmony with the Law of Love.

So, my friends, today let's realize the "light switch" is within us. The Power is always here. The illumination is ready when we are. We call forth the Power and release the light in our lives as we tune to the Voice of Love in our hearts and follow It's promptings.

Another Dimension

An ancient Chinese philosopher said,

> *"Once I dreamed I was Chuang Tzu dreaming I was a butterfly. But then I wondered, am I really a butterfly dreaming I'm Chuang Tzu?"*

Today, recognize that you are way more than you know you are. That you really are the free self. You really are the one that has the power and authority to be the co-author of the life you choose.

You are not just the limited being that sometimes we think we are. You are way more than that.

He said, "I dreamed I am this little person dreaming I was a butterfly and then I wondered was I really the butterfly dreaming I was this little person?"

So today we recognize that we are in the world, but as Jesus said, we are not of it. We come from another dimension and that dimension is one of freedom and power.

Present Now

The Center

This morning in my meditation, I began to think about the word "center." The word center is both a noun and a verb.

There is a center within each one of us of perfect peace. There is a center inside each one of us—Jesus called it the kingdom, a center within where we have access to infinite knowledge and wisdom.

There is a center within us where perfect guidance for our day can be found. There is a center within us of the experience of the companionship and the love and the healing and the forgiveness that is God's presence in our lives. To live from that center would bring a centering practice.

So our centering practice is to stay awake to what's really true. To practice seeing God hiding in every person and in every situation. To use every single moment as an opportunity to see that this present moment is the curriculum for my soul to remember who I am, then presence that in my daily life.

Today may each one of us find a deeper connection to the Center within, which is God's presence. By the way we live our lives this day, may it be a centering practice in everything we do.

Precious Gift of Life

I awoke on my birthday thinking about a Thornton Wilder play "Our Town," where the character Emily has passed on to the next realm. She is given the opportunity to relive one day of her life, so she picks her twelfth birthday and from the higher realm she views her life as she was at 12.

She comes down the stairs in the house where she was raised and her family is all busy doing what they do in the morning. The kids are playing, the father is reading the paper and the mother's in the kitchen cooking. There's the smell of the coffee and the sound of the toast being buttered. She hears the laughter and sees the flowers in the yard. The sun is shining through the window, and it's a little bit misty and as she sees life just happening all around her, she says this,

> *"Oh life! Does anyone ever really know how wonderful you are, while they are living it?"*

What a great question to ask ourselves. Does anyone know? Do I ever really know how wonderful my life is while I'm living it?

The Buddhists say that to have a human birth is the most precious gift there is. So for each one of us, today is a birth day. It is the day we're given, born to, a day of life. We get a chance to live our whole lifetime in minuscule today, one day at a time.

So I wish you a wondrous day remembering how wonderful life is while you're living it.

Calmness

James Allen wrote a classic book entitled, *As a Man Thinketh.*

There's a chapter in his book on serenity. I'd like to read you three sentences.

> *"Calmness of mind is one of the beautiful jewels of wisdom. When you are calm, having learned how to govern your own emotions, how to govern your own mind, you know how to access the gifts of the universe. Your prosperity increases, your opportunity to make a difference for good expands, and you live with a license of a higher order of being."*

Calmness of mind is one of the beautiful jewels of wisdom. Let us realize today that we can have calmness of mind.

In this present moment, we can be centered right in the center of the place within us where peace lives, in the midst of everything that is going on in our lives.

So we get a chance today to have a wonderful day of life practicing how to be calm in the presence of whatever is.

All Alone Together

I'm writing today from a park where I am with my granddaughter, Allie. We have long planned for a weekend where she and I would spend a few days together alone. She looked at me and she said, "We're all alone, together."

I thought about that. What would it be like if we could just walk through our days saying, "We're all alone together, with each other, with God, with this earth, with the land, with the sea, with the air, with all there is; we're all alone, together."

Not one of us is *really* ever alone. There is a Companionship and a Presence and a Power that is before us and behind us right now, above us and below us, all around us, and most of all, in us; speaking through the still, small voice.

Become aware of this, and it will help deepen and expand your life experience. We're never alone. We're all alone, together.

Awaken

Buddha was once asked who he was. He was asked, "Are you an angel?" and he said, "No." "Are you a saint?" and he said, "No." "Are you a great teacher?" and he said, "No." "Then who are you?" and he said, "I am awake."

So today is an opportunity for us to practice being more wakeful. To be awake to the miracle of aliveness. Instead of trying to find miracles, to be awake to the fact that everything around us is a miracle.

I am reminded that being awake means that some of the time we will get a little bit sleepy. But each one of us has an internal snooze alarm, which is simply this—our intention to stay awake.

So today we are awake to the miracle and we find it everywhere present.

Thank God It's Now

How many of us look forward to Friday?

To the freedom of the weekend where maybe you would get to sleep late, or have a special event planned with friends, or get something done around the house that you just don't have time for during the week. Maybe it means a getaway weekend.

We all start looking forward to Friday, and when it arrives, we say, "TGIF—Thank God It's Friday!"

What if we just lived with "Thank God it's NOW". What about a life where we just lean into thank God it's now. It's now!

So often we've been trained to live our lives for a future, for difference, for "if that can happen, then I'll relax, if that can happen then I'll be happy, if this could change then won't things be great."

Let's spend the day today, thanking God it's now; now, with the richness, the learning, the opportunity, the gifts right here and right now.

"TGIN." Thank God it's now.

Breathe and Know

I want to offer you a one-minute meditation by Thich Nhat Hanh, who is a master of present-moment living, of mindfulness. We can learn something from his one-minute meditation.

Breathing in, I know I'm breathing in.
(Breath in)
Breathing out, I know I'm breathing out.
(Breath out)

Breathing in, my breath grows deep.
Breathing out, by breath grows slow.

Breathing in, I calm my body.
Breathing out, I feel at ease.

Breathing in, I smile.
Breathing out, I release.

Breathing in, dwelling in the present moment.
Breathing out, it is a wonderful moment.

So when we bring ourselves to this present moment, we discover what's always true. In this moment is a miracle.

The Magic In 15 Minutes

May I introduce you to the possibility of what God can do in our lives with just fifteen minutes?

Today, somewhere in this wonderful day, carve out fifteen minutes just for you and your soul.

If the weather is nice enough where you are, go sit on your porch swing and rock for a few minutes and just see what comes to mind, what comes to heart, what comes to the appreciation of your feelings for being alive.

Or if this finds you needing to be indoors, then maybe just go sit in your favorite chair or exercise in a different way for fifteen minutes. Do some stretching or do some yoga.

I don't know what will occur to you, but I know if you give yourself the delicious gift of fifteen minutes just for you, you might just be surprised what God can do with fifteen minutes for your soul.

Prayer of Protection

James Dillet Freeman once wrote a prayer that has been spoken by hundreds of thousands of people, particularly when they have someone they'd like to pray for or an issue they're facing themselves.

So, right now as we create a miracle minute together, think of someone, or a situation that you know, could really use prayer right now—a sense of God's power and God's presence and God's peace—and bring that situation or that person to mind right now and join me in these thoughts.

> *The light of God surrounds you.*
> *The love of God enfolds you.*
> *The power of God protects you.*
> *The presence of God watches over you.*
> *Right where you are, God is.*

Now, bring yourself into that circle and feel that same energy for yourself because it's really true.

> *The light of God surrounds me.*
> *The love of God enfolds me.*
> *The power of God protects me.*
> *The presence of God is watching over me*
> *right now. Right where I am, God is.*

If you and I knew that this were really true and that everything in our lives was working for good right now, our whole bodies would relax. We'd feel a sense of peace. We would really know that we can let go and let God this day.

Holy Instant

In *A Course in Miracles* there is a line called the "Holy Instant." The Holy Instant is this very moment. All the possibility for a miracle, all the possibility for breakthrough, all the possibility for creativity, invention, healing, transformation—everything is contained in this Holy Instant.

Imagine walking through this day realizing that moment by moment you are in the Holy Instant of God, and there is nothing blocking you from anything that is God which is unlimited good, except our imagined sense of separation.

So, that means the only thing we really need to heal is our imagined sense of separation from God. Today we are in the Holy Instant. Today we are going to remember over and over again,

> *"I am in the Holy Instant of God.*
> *Right here, right now,*
> *I am in the Holy Instant of God!"*

Mindfulness

Will Hodges once said,

> *"Don't let yesterday take up too much of today."*

So today let's practice mindfulness. Bringing ourselves into the full presence of the gift of this day. "Don't let yesterday take up too much of today." So we let anything that's undone that can get handled today—we bring it to mind—and we handle it today.

But anything that is in our history that cannot be dealt with today, that cannot be shifted today or brought to a new perspective today or healed today; we just leave it alone.

We turn our attention to the present moment, to what we can do this day. And we don't let yesterday take up too much of today.

Holy Ground

There is a scripture that says,

> *"I was standing on holy ground and I did not know it."*

Let's ponder that. "I was standing on holy ground and I did not know it."

Now the holy ground is right where you are. Most of us walk through our days without even knowing it.

So for a moment, stand right where you are, fully present. Both feet on the ground, open the top part of your head and feel the power of life energy moving in and through you—connecting with Mother Earth. Her energy moving up through the soles of your feet, up your legs and your torso and across your shoulders and extending down through your hands and up through your head—calming, nurturing, renewing, restoring, every part of you.

I am standing on holy ground. For this moment, I do know it. May we extend this moment throughout our day and live a life where more and more we remember the miracle that we are truly on Holy Ground.

A Generous Spirit

BE the Blessing

What I know is that this day, every single one of us can BE the presence of God. Every one of us this day can BE the voice of God. Every single one of us this day can BE the support of God.

So let's pay attention because every one of us is on holy assignment. Every person who crosses our path today—from the grocery stores to the gas stations, to the people who pass us in traffic—let's consciously choose to BE the point of blessing. Extend a blessing in front of us and behind us and above us and below us and all around us. There is no one with whom we come in contact this day, not even those who we think about, who will not move into the field of blessing because we are the point from where the blessing is coming.

So go deep within your heart right now. Is there anything you could be doing today that is more important? No matter what it is that's on your "to do" list, resolve that your major "TO BE" list is to BE the blessing. We can be the change point in the world, a blessing to this day.

Go First

I remember a story about a mom making pancakes for her sons. Tommy was four and Billy was two and she was making those Mickey Mouse pancakes where you pour one circle for the head and two smaller circles on top of it to make the ears.

As she flipped the pancakes, one of them got messed up while the other stayed intact. The older brother, Tommy, looked at the good one and said, "Ohhh, I want that pancake." Mother looked at Tommy and said, "Tommy, Jesus would give his little brother the better pancake." So Tommy looked at his mother and said, "Ah, it's okay. Today Billy can be Jesus. Let him be Jesus."

I was thinking how tempting it is for us in our lives to not want to be the one who goes first. To not want to be the one who keeps giving. To hear the Golden Rule but see our application of it waiver at times because of what's going on in our lives.

So today, what if we just made the decision that we're going to be the one who goes first all day long? We might be the person who buys coffee for the person behind us in line at a coffee shop. We might be the person who pays the toll for the person behind us in line. We might be the person who reaches out once more to a friend who hasn't been able to or has been unwilling to reach out to us.

What if we just make a decision this day to presence on this planet the Golden Rule? We will be the place where that gold is not only found, but delivered.

Everything is a Miracle

I am reminded of a saying by Albert Einstein:

> *"There are only two ways to approach life. Take your day and imagine that every single part of that day is a miracle because either everything is a miracle or nothing is a miracle." Then he said, "and from everything I've ever learned, everything is a miracle."*

There is no distinguishment and no decision. Either it is all a miracle, of none of it is a miracle.

So make your decision, how will this week be for you? What if we lived a week of our lives—just one week—where we really amplified our vision, our seeing, our hearing, believing that everything, everything is a miracle.

One of the best ways we move in the stream of awareness that keeps our eyes and heart open to the miracle is to practice making someone's day. Whether it's the grocery clerk or the gas station attendant or whomever you come in contact, let that person be the person that for a moment, see if you can make their day.

Notice how that adds up to making your day one of a real miracle.

Make the World a Better Place

I read a quote this morning that said,

> *"Whenever someone does something nice for someone else, the entire world becomes a better place for all of us."*

Whenever someone does something nice for someone else, the entire world becomes a better place for all of us.

Deep down I know that's true. So today, remember also the saying about doing random acts of kindness; (I imagine they shouldn't be so random). But nevertheless, let's each effort today in the best way that efforting is—which is simply a non-pushing, an allowing—that we will recognize the moments when we really could do something, say something, or smile something nice for someone else. We really can collectively make this world a better place today.

Margaret Mead said,

> *"Never doubt that a small group of committed people can change the world. In fact, it is the only thing that ever has."*

So today we make the world a better place. It's our miracle minute.

Thank You For Being a Friend

There was a famous song once that said, "Thank you for being a friend." When we really add up our blessings, we find our friends are at the top of the list. We know they have really made a difference in our lives.

Right now, think of someone who has made a difference in your life through their caring, their showing up, their advice. Somehow they have been a friend to you in this journey of human life.

So today, think of at least one friend who you can contact—and make it happen today—call them up or send them a note, but take the action today to thank them for being a friend.

Thank you for being a friend. To all of you reading this, I send you the blessings of the friendship that we have through sharing these moments together and extend that blessing through you to all the people who have made a difference in your life.

The Good Samaritan

I was reflecting on the story of the Good Samaritan. Most of you know that story. Jesus tells of how a Good Samaritan helps another one in need. It is unexpected that he would help, because he is not of the same lineage, he's not of the same tribe, and he's not even of the same group.

But, the Samaritan sees that person in need and in a moment reaches out to help in a really healthy way. He makes sure the person gets help, but he doesn't take him home with him. He makes sure the person gets help, but he continues with his own life. He makes sure the person gets help in a way that is expansive and life-giving for everyone concerned.

Then Jesus said, "Now go and do likewise." That last line I think is important for us, perhaps even today.

Somebody's going to show up today in our lives and we get to be the one who actually is the one to "go and do likewise." We get to be the Good Samaritan when we discover somebody today who needs our help.

Let's be the one who gives the help in a way that works for all of life, including our own. This day let's find out where we're supposed to be the Good Samaritan.

Someone Needs a Prayer Today

A friend of mine sings a song called "Someone Needs a Prayer Today."

What if today every one of us just considered this idea and practice to be our miracle minute? Who are the people right now who need some prayer today? What if we become part of their team of support by lifting them up, holding them up and supporting them by seeing them in their wholeness?

Whenever Jesus was involved in healing, he looked at the problem, he looked at the being who was in a circumstance, but he held the image and evoked the hologram, "whole-o-gram" of their wholeness.

Right now, it might be a child, it might be a senior person, it might be somebody at your workplace; I don't know who that may be. Let the Holy Spirit prompt you with an idea. Become part of the prayer team right now for that person. In your mind, lift them up. Hold them up. Help set them free.

We know that whatever we're doing for each other, we're actually doing for ourselves. So today, it will be a miracle minute every time you stop and pray for someone you know who needs a prayer.

Significance

I recently watched a Spiritual Cinema film called *The Serious Business of Happiness*. One of the men in that film, Father Matthew Kelly, who is a progressive priest in the Catholic church, gave a really powerful comment about the difference between success and significance.

Every one of us has been trained to try to create success, but there is a different kind of satisfaction, fulfillment, and completion that comes when we instead make a life of significance.

The only way to make a life of significance is to pay attention to what we're doing to help others. As we pay attention to what we're doing to help others, we take the feeling of needing to get things done and transform it into a feeling that the whole Universe is in support of what we're about.

In truth, the Universe cares about every single one of us. So today, let's take this one day and instead of trying to have the day be a success, let's make it a day of significance.

Vision Keepers

I want to remind you what it means to be a vision keeper. The German philosopher Goethe said,

> *"Treat people as if they were what they ought to be and you help them to become what they are capable of being."*

We are a vision keeper for anyone we know when we hold them to the highest point of view in our minds of what's possible for them.

We hold a vision for them as others are holding a vision for us. We remind each other when we've lost sight of our vision. We remind each other when we've fallen down that it's really more uncomfortable to stay down than to get up again. We think of each other in the highest point of view.

There's somebody you know today who could really benefit from a phone call or a card from you. Take a moment today and lift up someone else to the highest point of view. Tell them, "What I know about you..." and then say the words that you know can make a difference in helping them know and remember the very best about themselves.

Be a Vision Keeper today.

Truly Helpful

A Course in Miracles has a wonderful line that says,

> *"I am here only to be truly helpful. I am here to represent the one who sends me. I don't have to worry about what to say or what to do because the one who sends me will direct me. I am content to go where I am directed."*

Let's practice walking through this day realizing I am here only to be truly helpful. I am here to re-present or bring in, through human form, the God who sends me, the God who is the essence of the aliveness that I am. I am here to represent God on earth.

I don't have to worry. I don't have to figure it all out. What a relief that is. My shoulders can relax. My forehead can relax. I can let go of the tension. I don't really have to figure it all out because the one who sends me will direct me moment-by-moment.

So I am content to go where I am directed knowing I don't go alone. If I could remember just for even a part of this day Who walks with me, I'd never be afraid again.

I am here only to be truly helpful.

Sow Your Good

Jesus once said,

> *"Sometimes we sow in one field and harvest in another."*

What's he saying? He's saying that the good we give can never be erased. While at times it looks like we may have lost something or given more than we should have; someone took advantage of us or we didn't get what we thought was ours; what he is saying is don't look to any specific field—like the particular work you're doing or the particular bank account or the particular relationship. But, give and give generously of yourself and your love and your talent and you can trust your harvest is assured.

What he's saying explains the way the Universe works. The reward is yours and it will come to you in ways that are unexpected—absolutely unexpected.

It was Emerson who said, "God always plays with loaded dice." Both were speaking about the way the Universe works, and you can trust that Universe to bring you your good in response to the good you put out.

Go ahead and sow your good today.

Compassionate Breathing

I want to invite you to pause right where you are and take a deep breath and to practice what his Holiness the Dali Lama calls "Compassionate Breathing."

Take a breath in, hold it, and then breathe out compassion for our entire world—for every person, for our family in Iraq, our family in South America, our family in Africa, our family in the United States and Asia and the Nordic countries, our family in the neighborhoods we live in, our family that we know, and the family within ourselves.

So again, we take a deep breath in and we breathe out compassion. We place compassion right in the center of our hearts for all the decision makers today who are making decisions about the future choices of our country and countries around the world, and we ask that this compassion bring its wisdom and its healing.

Then we breathe in one more time and breathe out compassion for the decision maker in us, the one who decides how we will use this precious day of life. May it be used wisely and with love.

Guardians

In my office where I'm writing this message, there is a poster hanging on my wall that I love very much. I read it just about every time I come into my office.

I wanted to invite you into the prayer that's on this poster with me today. The poster has four figures. They're people without faces symbolizing every single one of us can become part of this, and the words on the poster say,

> *"Guardians. I swear I will not dishonor my soul with hatred but offer myself humbly as a guardian of nature, as a healer of misery, as a messenger of wonder, as an architect of peace."*

I swear I will not dishonor myself with hatred, but offer myself humbly as a guardian of nature, as a healer of misery, as a messenger of wonder, as an architect of peace.

So today may we each offer ourselves humbly to all that we can be.

Where Two or More are Gathered

For many, many years, I've had a prayer partner that I meet with on Thursday mornings. Often we meet at six o'clock in the morning by phone and we'll spend an hour together praying for one another, supporting one another, reminding each other about what we really know is true about the other.

Jesus said, "whenever two or more of you are gathered in my name," meaning in the spirit of the Divine Love, in the spirit of seeing each other in our true nature, in the spirit of the Christ mind; "I am in your midst."

There is a power released, a synergy experienced, a potency revealed that is way beyond anything any one of us can get to on our own. I don't know exactly how this works; I just know that it does work.

So I encourage you, before you put your head down on the pillow tonight, call someone you care about and just say to them, "You know, I was just thinking about you today, and what I know about you is you are a person of power. What I know about you is you are a person of creativity. What I know about you is you are a person who's an overcomer."

Give that person a burst of energy from your Christ self, your Divine mind, that part of you that knows the Truth. I promise you it will open a doorway to where you will feel more powerful, more loving, more secure yourself.

Random Acts of Kindness

One minute can change our day.

Do you remember a bumper sticker from a movement years ago that said, "Practice random acts of kindness and senseless beauty."

Many people began to try it out, but then it faded into the background.

What if today was "Random Acts of Kindness Day?" What if we took advantage of every chance we got to practice a random kindness?

If we're at a toll booth we might pay for the person behind us; if we're in a coffee shop we might offer to pay for the for the person behind us, but not tell them—just leave the money with the cashier and then walk away.

Notice what happens to your day as you practice random acts of kindness. Let's try it and see what happens!

Do All You Can

I am reminded of Nkosi Johnson's words, the African boy who died at 12 years old of AIDS. After his parents, his brothers and sisters had died, he decided to give a message to the world. He started out speaking to everyone he could find. His message gathered momentum and he was taken to speak in front of large audiences in South Africa, in Europe, with Larry King, and even on Oprah.

This young boy put a face on AIDS. He spoke out to everyone because he wanted them to not be afraid and to seek treatment. But, he was also calling on a world of people who might do what they can themselves, each one of us, to take a step this day to make this world a better place, in some way.

It might be helping a person. It might be a smile. It might be an extra kindness— perhaps a random act of kindness where someone never even knows of our acts. There is something you and I can do this day to make this world a better place. There is an impulse for that within us. His message is this:

> *"Do all you can with what you have, in the time you have, in the place you are. Do all you can."*

Do all you can with what you have, in the time you have, in the place you are. Do all you can.

P.S. Two friends, whose singing duo is called "Devotion" wrote a song about Nkosi called, "Do All You Can." It's great!

A Grateful Heart

Grateful In All Things

The apostle Paul wrote from a dark, dank prison—a really horrendous place, not prisons like we know today. From that place, he wrote these words. "I have learned this one thing in life."

So if someone were to say to you today "what's the one thing you've learned in life?" What would you say? Paul says, "I have learned this one thing in life." I have learned this. "That whatever state I find myself, therein to be grateful." Whatever condition in which I find myself, therein to be grateful.

Now he's saying something very important for us in the experience of the amplified living that comes from a state of gratitude. He's saying I'm not grateful for being in this prison. I'm not grateful for the experience. I'm grateful ***in*** the experience. We're all in the condition of experience which is the out-picturing of the life that we're living. We call it our situations, our circumstances, our conditions.

No matter what the conditions, be grateful because gratitude is transformative. Gratitude lifts our perspective. Gratitude changes the vibratory field in such a way that we begin to have access to the field of all possibilities.

So no matter what state, no matter what condition in which we find ourselves right now, we just simply move to a state of gratitude, "therein to be grateful." We begin to open up, allow, ask for, and experience the miracle that is here for every one of us this day. No matter what circumstance, therein today, I am practicing being grateful.

Our Guidance System

Pause where you are right now and feel your aliveness. Just feel your aliveness. Feel your body. If you have shoes on, feel the shoes on your feet and the clothing on your skin and the breeze caressing your exposed skin. Thank God for this holy temple called your body.

For a moment, notice that you have thoughts. You can choose your thoughts because you are a co-creator with God. Give thanks right now for the power that you have to choose your own thoughts and the capacity to exercise that power.

Right now notice that you have feelings, which are one of your intelligence systems because they tell you when you're on track. You know, because you feel good when you're on track and feel bad when you're off track. That part of our guidance system is our feelings.

So right now we give thanks for our body, for our thoughts, for our emotions—all of which are God's gift to us as part of this wondrous, wondrous, holy gift called a human life.

What Matters Most

Almost all of us will remember where we were on September 11, 2001. As shocking and difficult as that news was, and what it might bring in the ensuing years, there were some powerful lessons given that day.

A lesson that struck a chord with millions of us watching that day was the recognition that when there were people in burning buildings and planes about to crash, those people were not busy making phone calls to their stockbroker.

No, they were doing something else. They were calling the people they loved because when it all comes down to it, there is really only one thing that matters—and that one thing is love.

So don't miss a day telling the people you care that you love and appreciate them. Today, let's take a deep breath of life and appreciate the opportunity we have to express our caring, to feel our gratitude, and to live this life that is a precious, precious gift.

We pause for a moment and feel that gratitude, and we take it forward throughout our whole day.

Gifts On Loan

There is a teaching story about a group of scientists who having discovered the secrets of cloning decided they would have a conference with God and tell God, He/She was no longer needed. Yes, God had created humanity and all of life, in fact, from the very dust of the earth. But now, science had taken over the job and God could retire.

So the top scientists in the world gathered together and called God to a conference. Having been told that He/She was no longer required, God said, "Explain this to me." The scientists said, "We now know how to make life out of dust ourselves." God said to them, "Well then, okay, you go ahead and show me how you can do that." So they reached down for some dirt. And God said, "Uh, uh, uh, get your own dirt."

I love that story because it just reminds us how we get confused at times and think things really belong to us—even our life itself. We begin to forget at times how precious the gift is of our daily life.

In everything we call ours—even our children, our spouses, our friends—they're gifts on loan from the Universe. How precious it is to have these gifts in our lives this day. To have eyes to see and ears to hear. This day is a gift and it all belongs to the One who sources all of this.

So today let's walk around in deep appreciation of the real heritage that we have, that we get to walk in the abundance of the gift of this human life.

Praise Power

Many years ago in the early 1970s, a minister came to my hometown of Beaverton, Oregon; he was one of the first people who really introduced me to the experience of the presence of God as an Abiding Presence, as a Companion.

Some of the things he said just opened the doors to my self. I felt like I'd been in a dark attic and all of a sudden I found my way through the whole household of selves into the door opening. And here was the Universe of love waiting for me to find my way—through the practice of connection to God's presence.

One of the practices of this connection is a simple one called "Praise Power." Praise Power is where we look for things to praise and then say "thank you. "

Look for things to praise in life and say "thank you." Look for things to praise in our friends and say "thank you." Look for things to praise in nature and say "thank you." Look for things to praise in our kids, in our spouse, our co-workers, in the job we have.

The human mind so often wants to look for what's missing and what's wrong. When we instead go to the mind that tells us what's good, what's here now and celebrate that, we find a doorway and access to a Universe of Love's Presence.

So today let's practice Praise Power. Let's look for the good and praise it.

Your Divine Plan

Imagine that the Universe has got your day perfectly designed right now so that in every single moment, exactly what you need to know, exactly what you need for inspiration, exactly what you need for the answers to everything you're longing for and searching for is right where you are.

There will be people that will show up today, books that will jump off the shelves—in a sense—if you look at them. Everything single thing you need is right where you are.

So let's take our universal eyes. Let's take our eyes of believing that God is present everywhere to our day. Let's say, "Thank you God for the signs and the signals that you are sending me this day. Thank you for all the ways you are showing up in my life this day. Thank you that everything I need to know is right where I am today."

When we take those eyes and those ears to our day, it always turns into miracle minute after miracle minute.

Where's Your Focus?

Have you ever noticed that what you focus on, you begin to see more of? If you're hungry, you start noticing everything there is to eat. If you are wanting to buy a new red sports car, all of a sudden you see little red sports cars everywhere you're looking. What we focus on expands.

Most of us have a tendency to focus on what's missing and what's wrong, because we want to fill what's missing and we want to fix what's wrong.

Another way of doing this—actually a way that is much, much more powerful—is for us to focus on what is right and what is here. Because in truth, God is here. So really there is nothing wrong except our perception. What we focus on expands.

So right now, in your life, what can you be grateful for? What can you appreciate?

Focus on appreciation and gratitude this day and you will find that you are attracting to you by the Law of Attraction, much, much more of the good that's already yours by Divine right.

It's All Good

At the end of each day of creation in the Biblical story of how the Genesis of the world came about, God said, "Let there be . . ." and then said, "and it is good." And, it is good, and it is good.

So, right now what if every single thing that was happening in your life was actually good? What if everything in your life was part of a good that you can't even comprehend or begin to believe but can trust in anyway?

There is a Hafiz poem that asks,

> *"What if you were playing chess with the most intelligent, wise Being that ever existed in the entire universe, and that Being wanted you to become master of the game? Where would every piece be on the chess board but exactly where it needed to be to help you become the master of the game?"*

Well every part of your life is just like that, and my life too. It is set up in such a way that we have the maximum opportunity to become fully realized as the son or daughter of God that we really are. To become master of the game of life.

So today we say, "It is good." And we recognize that in that gratitude, everything in our life begins to expand.

Thank You God

I remembered Meister Eckhardt's saying where he said,

> *"If you only had one prayer, let it be 'Thank you God.' "*

Over the last year and a half I have been practicing a chosen gratitude—a way of being in the world that is choosing to be grateful, not in the absence of circumstances or problems, but in the presence of circumstances and problems.

In the midst of that, the blessings that are here for each one of us have become more apparent for me. I realize that through this practice, I have given myself perhaps one of the greatest of all gifts of Spirit. Yet I feel like I have just barely cracked open the door.

So I invite you today, my friend, to give yourself the gift of starting right now for the next year of your life, to practice the choosing of a new gratitude. A chosen gratitude where several times a day you pause to just simply say, "Thank you God for my life—for all of it... for all of it."

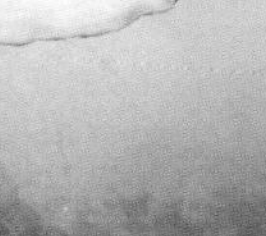

A Merry Heart

Not long ago I was speaking with a group of people who have been doing the recent research on gratitude from a scientific point of view.

All the new research from Harvard and Penn State and every other prestigious university that is doing research on the power of gratitude—what it does to the brain, the pheromones, all the good chemicals that are released, what happens in our bodies and our immune system—proves that there is scientific evidence that gratitude has positive medical benefits.

It shows that choosing to live from a place of gratitude, paying attention to what you can be grateful for, giving thanks on a daily basis, repeatedly and regularly is really good for our health.

More than that, it moves us into a stream of our genius. People who are grateful attract to themselves more ideas, more support, more resources. Their relationships work better. I think that maybe scripture knew what it was saying to us thousands of years ago when it was written, "A merry heart doeth good, like medicine."

So my friend, let's choose today to live from a merry heart. Instead of putting our attention on what's wrong, we put our attention on what's right and we say "Thank you God for this life. Thank you God for this day." Make it a merry one!

A Measurable Shift

Recent research tells each one of us that there is a whole chemical shift that happens in our bodies when we decide—and then determine—to live from gratitude.

It makes our immune system much more potent. It makes us able to keep ourselves in a healthy state and no matter what we're around; it is almost as if a bubble of protection is around us. It is not something we can manufacture by pretending, but it is something we can create by entering into a field of gratitude.

There is also new research behind that that says speaking your gratitude out loud actually amplifies the positive affects of holding gratitude. It is one thing to think gratitude and feel gratitude, but when we express gratitude it amplifies the positive results not only for ourselves, but for the others to whom we express this gratitude. When we live from gratitude, everything works better.

So my friends, this day let's each practice thinking, feeling, and speaking our gratitude.

Thank You

The woman who wrote the book, *The Secret*, Rhonda Byrnes, writes about gratitude.

She said that when she realized the true power of gratitude, she began to start her day with a practice that infused it with a whole different frequency of energy—an energy that is much more attractive to the ideas, the inspiration, the support and the resources for our dreams. That energy is a magnitude of gratitude.

One of her practices was that with every step, she would put her left foot down and say "Thank" and put her right foot down and say "You." "Thank you." "Thank you" with each step.

For two minutes at a time she practiced just saying "thank you" with the steps she was taking as she did her laundry, as she went to the grocery store, as she walked through her office. "Thank you. Thank you. Thank you."

So today, let us move into a whole new stream of good by moving to a whole new frequency of gratitude. "Thank you."

Inner Listening

Out of the Silence

I was sitting with some friends this morning and we were discussing some of the best music we've ever heard. Among us, one of the things we had loved was Van Morrison's album, "Hymns to the Silence."

It reminded me of a teaching story where the master says to his students, "What do the musician and the artist have in common with the mystic?" They all give up and finally the master says, "The musician and the artist realize that the finest speech does not come from the tongue, it comes out of the silence."

So today, may we incorporate a new listening of what the silence; speaking through nature, speaking between the lines, speaking between the sounds, even speaking between the beats of our own heart, is speaking to us. Between the breath in, the breath out, in the pause, in the silence, is the voice of God. In the silence is Everywhere Present. It doesn't require external silence. It requires a listening for the internal Voice that is always with us, particularly the Universe's love for us right here and right now.

So today, we listen to the silence.

The One Thing

I once heard a question asked that I think is a really important question to ask ourselves every now and then. Here's the question:

> *"What one thing am I not doing, that if I did do, would greatly improve my life six months from now?"*

What one thing am I not doing that if I did do would vastly improve my life six months from now? And then listen, because the "You" of you might have a very important message for you.

It might be to walk thirty minutes a day. It might be to listen deeper five minutes a day. It might be a hundred other things, but the "You" of you, the I Am that is breathing you and calling you, has a message for each one of us when we listen.

"What one thing am I not doing that if I did do would vastly improve my life six months from now?" Let's listen to what that inner voice might say to us today.

Flow

When I drove across the Continental Divide I was reminded how on one side of the divide, things flow one way and on the other side they flow another.

I think there is a moment in our lives where we cross our own Continental Divide. Where we make a decision to really listen to that still, small voice and we realize that if we follow that voice and pay attention to that voice, things flow in a whole different direction.

When we operate under our own power, it really isn't power, it is force. So let us be reminded to take no other gods before Me. That "Me" that is that still small voice within you. It is our highest authority, our greatest strength, our deepest peace, and everything we would hope for.

We cross that Continental Divide today, each one of us, with a decision to listen moment by moment.

Best Thinking

For many, many years I've known that some of my best thinking actually happens in the shower. Ideas come to me because the distraction of the external world in my focus of awareness. I'm actually able to access those higher ideas.

Sometimes when I'm getting dressed in the morning or doing my hair, ideas come to me and I'm able to sort and discover and listen in. I think it is very important for us to discover the routinely active ways we have to discover, listen in to, and find our very best thinking.

Remember your thinking comes from not only from your intellect, but from your intuition. There is a GPS, God Positioning System, that's inside you that knows exactly your next step, knows exactly what would bring you the most joy, the most aliveness, the most peace; but you and I have to be accessible to that, available to that, and willing to receive that.

One of the best clues is to know the key that opens the door to our own best thinking. So today, just listen in. Notice your day, but pay attention to your own best thinking. It's God's voice and it's speaking to you.

Beingness

When did the day begin for you today? Historically and Biblically the next day begins when we go to bed the night before. When we close down our day and we take a review of the day.

We look back over our day and if there are amends to make, we set an intention of making them the next day. If there are things to correct or change or lessons to be learned, we settle our day. Then we go to sleep keeping in mind what we would like to create the next day. It's not just our "to do" list, it's our "to be" list.

The best time to intentionalize our "to be" list is when we're quiet. What would I really like to be? What would I like to bring into my life? What would I like to contribute?

So guess what, your day can begin right now. For the rest of this day, what would you like to be? Not just what you want to do? What do you want to be?

Right now this is your moment; let it be a shining one.

Touch the Leader in You

Max DuPree wrote a book on leadership. Chapter 1 begins with a question. "What is leadership?" The first line of the book says this, "The first responsibility of a leader is to define reality. "

A leader, a real leader, accesses reality internally, not externally. There are circumstances and there are facts, but reality is the capacity to define reality and call forth what you want to make real. A real leader accesses reality from the internal world—not from the external world.

So our real job is to spend at least five minutes in the morning quietly going within and accessing the reality we want to create and then sending forth those images. We'll be holding images anyway for the day. Send forth the images of the possibility of doing what can make our lives, our world, a better world.

There is nothing higher to do with your day than taking those five minutes to access reality, touching the leader that is within you to define the reality you're called to bring.

The Other Side of the Boat

Do you remember the story in the Bible about the disciples who had been fishing and fishing and fishing in the Sea of Galilee, yet getting nothing?

Jesus said to them, "Take your nets and put them on the right side of the boat." They do that and their nets come in so full that they are breaking under the weight of all the fish they're bringing up. The whole bottom of their boat now becomes filled with the fish that they were trying so desperately to get before that.

Now it doesn't make sense to the logical mind that on one side of the boat—in the very same water—a net is catching nothing and on the other side of the boat, there is so much that it almost breaks the net.

What is Jesus really saying to us? That there is a "right way." In the right side of our nature is our creative self, is our intuitive self, is the Self that can really hear the Voice of God.

So today we go to the "right" side of the boat of our life and we ask what would God place in the net of our own activity, our own thinking, our own being—and we listen.

That Inner Voice

Have you ever had an intuition, had a voice speak to you, or a sense of knowing that says something like, "Turn here, don't go down that road" or "bring your umbrella today." And, have you ever said back to that voice when it speaks to you, "You know what, I don't really need my umbrella," or "I'm going this way," and then to find out that voice really knew more than you did?

The great thing about having a Higher Power is that it is Higher. Our challenge, in our spiritual practice, is to submit to, harness ourselves to, and really be in relationship with that Voice.

Do it in an honoring way, be humble before the Divinity that lives and is always seeking expression through us.

I can't tell you how many times I knew something, but didn't pay attention and then paid the price.

So today, may we each, let this be a day of listening to and following our Inner Voice.

Silence

The Navajo had a special way of speaking. They spoke and then they would be silent. They would state an idea and then they would be silent.

They believed that the silence was more informative than the spoken word and unless they allowed the silence, they would never know the full meaning of the words.

So today as you move through your day, as you hear ideas, as you think and speak your ideas, and as you're working through the many aspects of what this day's life is about; take some moments and listen into the silence. Create some spaces between the ideas and ask the silence to speak to you about your life this day.

I believe that as we do that, each one of us will find that we are part of something that is already a miracle just awaiting our discovery.

Have a miraculous day discovering the gift of your silence—the silence that is always with you and always for you.

God Is Everywhere

I was told that Meister Eckhart was once asked how to describe God, and he said this:

> *"God is a circle whose center is everywhere and whose circumference or ending is nowhere."*

God is a circle whose center is everywhere. Right where you are is the center of God's presence, God's power, God's love, God's wisdom, God's peace, God's grace. You are the center of all that is God. There is no place you can go, no experience you can have that would be outside the circle of God's presence and power and love and wisdom and grace.

When we know that even the earthworm is at the center of God and that the robin also sees itself to be at the center of God, we see God is everywhere present – there is nothing missing today. All we need do is tune in, get quiet for a moment and build a feeling of appreciation. Then we have access to everything that is our Divine right.

God is a circle whose center is everywhere and whose circumference or ending is nowhere. Right where you are, you are at the center of God.

The Inner Knower

I was having breakfast with my stepson, Michael, the other day. He's a young adult now, facing a very, very important choice in his life.

He said, "You know Mom, I'm reminded of that Robert Frost poem, 'Two roads diverged in a woods and I…' " He said, before he closed the prayer, "You know he's going to say that he took the road less traveled by—because one of those paths that is diverging is a well-known path and lots of people have gone down that path. The other is not well worn and there is some exploring to do and there may be more difficulties and things to get out of the way. But how do you know which is the well-known path? How do you know the one that really is the path of your soul?"

What I told Michael and what I reminded myself in that moment, is that there is a place inside of us called our Knower, and the Knower knows.

You can trust your own life force. Listen for that Voice and pay attention and it will make ALL the difference.

So today, and every day of our lives, the paths are many, and they are diverging. Let us pick the path of our Soul.

Advance in Faith

There's a quote that says,

> *"The one who waits until all the facts are known before making a decision spends their life on standstill."*

The one who waits until all the facts are known before making a decision spends their life on standstill.

Today you and I are going to be doing some things. We're creating a day of life today. So let's listen to the still small voice, go to the edge of the light we see, and move with the highest guidance we've got; giving ourselves the opportunity to do some things that absolutely work out and some things that turn out to be mistakes—because that is the learning process.

In that process we discover more of who we are and who God is. This is the day that God has made, let us rejoice and be glad in it. He or she who waits until all the facts are known, spends their life in a standstill. That will not be us today!

From Superheros and Fairy Tales

Follow the Yellow Brick Road

Do you remember the scene in the classic 1939 film "The Wizard of Oz" after the tornado comes and Dorothy finds herself in a strange land? All she wants to do is find her way home.

She meets characters along the way who help her in her quest to get home. The first are little beings, little voices that say, "Follow the yellow brick road. Follow the yellow brick road." Follow the light. Go to the edge of the light you see and follow it.

So today, the decision making we're doing, and the choices that we're choosing become the markers by which our life is guided.

Let us each look for the yellow brick road. What is the most light-providing and life-giving choice we can make for our lives every moment this day?

Today, let's follow the yellow brick road.

Believing the Impossible

I was thinking this morning about something that was written in *Alice in Wonderland*, where the Queen says to Alice, "Alice, tell me what happened tomorrow." Alice says, "I can't tell you what happened tomorrow. It's impossible to tell you what happened tomorrow."

And the Queen says to Alice, "My dear, I would dare say you simply have not had much practice. Why, when I was your age, I used to practice believing ten impossible things before breakfast. And besides that Alice, it's a pretty poor memory that only works in one direction."

What Lewis Carroll was telling us is that we have capacities of imagination and visualization that are ours to use or to ignore. When the human mind is tempting us to say, "Well that's impossible," he's telling us to practice believing beyond the boundaries of what we've known.

So if you could choose what your life would be like six months from now, tell me what happened tomorrow. If you went beyond the boundaries of what you've known, what might you imagine and be willing to claim?

It might seem impossible, but this is the part I really like. Today let's begin to practice believing in some impossible things, and then release God in our life to do what only God can do…the impossible.

I Am What I Am

I was thinking about childhood and the amazing motto that the cartoon character Popeye had. "I am what I am and that's all that I am." Then, of course, he added, "I'm Popeye the sailor man."

I am what I am and that's all that I am. That "All that I am" is plenty enough. The I that I am is all that I am.

All the stories, all the events, all the circumstances are not who you are. They're just stories. They're just circumstances. They're just the events.

But who you are is a son, is a daughter of the Most High. Be reminded of *A Course in Miracles*, and its quote that says to you, "Oh son, oh daughter of God, if you only knew who walks with you this day, you could never be afraid again."

So through this day just remind yourself, "I am what I am and what I am is a son of God. What I am is a daughter of God. I am what I am and that's all that I am and that's more than enough."

The Wisdom of Yoda

Do you remember in the Star Wars movies the great wisdom that came through the little character, Yoda? One of his wisdom teachings has stayed with me a long time.

Luke is asking the wise one, "How do I know the right decision to make?" Among all the many decisions, how do I know the one that will be "with the Force" or in the will of God? How do I know the right decision to make?

Yoda looks at him and says,

"You will know through the peace and calm."

You will know you're on the right track when you're not feeling frantic, when you're not feeling anxious, when you're not struggling with different parts of yourself. When you get to the right answer and the right decision that is yours, there will be a peace and calm that will show up within you and radiate from you.

So, as we make decisions today, may we look for that peace and calm that is the confirmation that we are in the will of God—in the Tao, or in the way of things.

Let us turn to that peace and calm as our compass and our comfort.

Expecto Patronum

Do you remember in the Harry Potter series the training for how to deal with dementors; or doubt, or that which would constrict or constrain us—that which would cause us to live in our littleness?

The wizard's training is to take the magic wand in your hand, think of the happiest thought you can think and then say, "expecto patronum." When you say that, it is as if there is a new vibration that emerges and it absolutely re-establishes that person's safety and balance.

So if there is any doubt today that you're experiencing, anything, in any part of you—and there is going to be, because we're in a human experience today—let us practice our own wizard's training and think of the happiest thought we can think in the moment when the doubt tries to gain entrance and control.

Expecto perfection, expecto a higher power to be at work, expecto . . . and then you and I choose to move into an expectation of our good by first thinking the happiest thought we can, secondly, casting a strong energy clearing our way. Expecto Patronum!

Think Fourth Dimensionally

I recently took my granddaughter Allie to Universal Studios. We visited the "Back to the Future" attraction. Many of you will remember the "Back to the Future" movies with Doc Brown and Marty McFly.

As "Doc Brown" was smiling and waving at Allie, I was talking to her about a scene in the movie where Marty feels completely stymied by a problem and sees no way around it. Doc Brown says to him, "Marty, you're not thinking fourth dimensionally."

As soon as he begins to think fourth dimensionally—or at a new level—all of a sudden ideas come to him and then he's got the answer.

Thinking fourth dimensionally means thinking outside the problem. Instead of thinking how big the problem is, start thinking how big God is and then tell the problem about your big God.

Ideas start to come to us when we realize we really do have a capacity of thinking that gives us an access to achieving anything we choose. So, what do we choose?

You have a day right now that you're holding in your hands, which is yours to craft and shape and mold any way you choose. The day isn't contained by what's in it; it's contained by how you think about it.

Let's think fourth dimensionally today.

Mirror Love's Presence

It was the English author Albert Beach, who when writing the English lyrics for a French song, could hear the couple next door engaged in a verbal free-for-all.

Heated words bounced through the thin walls and writing a love lyric seemed nearly impossible.

He started to re-read *Through the Looking Glass*, the story of Alice in Wonderland. He got no further than Alice's remark to her kitten,

> *"First there's a room you can see through the glass that's just the same as our drawing room, only things go the other way."*

Beach started mirroring the neighbor's hate words into opposites. His lyrics were at the publishers the very next day.

Instead of framing what he was hearing as the hate words next door, he wrote this: "I wish you bluebirds in the Spring to give your heart a song to sing and then a kiss but more than this, I wish you love."

So whatever negative is happening in your life, you can mirror the opposite. You can mirror the level that is more reflective of love's presence. There is no more powerful message than that. And right now, I wish you love.

True Perception

I saw a Peanuts cartoon one time where Lucy and Charlie Brown were having a conversation.

Lucy was looking out the window and Charlie Brown came to look out the window with her and he says, "Oh my gosh, look at all of the spots on the window. Every corner has a spot." And Lucy says to him, "Charlie Brown, don't you know that windows are for looking through, not at."

It was a very metaphysical comment on our ability to see through conditions, our ability to see through difficulties, our ability to see through problems, our ability to see through circumstances.

Human life is filled with circumstances and situations some of which we call problems, some of which we call opportunities. But, there is an ability each one of us has called our "true perception," to be able to see through and see the truth and see that every single thing in our lives has a gift just waiting to be unwrapped.

So today, rather than looking at our problems, let's look through our problems and recognize the love and the power and the glory of life, right where we are.

Find Your Way Home

Do you remember in The Wizard of Oz when Dorothy is looking and looking for how to find her way home?

Finally, from the voice that is the voice of the wise one showing up as Glinda, she's told that she's always had the power to go home. She's always had it with her. She just didn't know it.

Each one of us can be reminded that no matter where we are, no matter where we find ourselves, and no matter what we're facing—each one of us has always had the power. The power to go to that place in ourselves where we are connected to a Presence and a Power and a Peace that is greater than anything we're facing. Jesus called this the Kingdom that is within.

So let's spend this day centered in a place inside ourselves. This is our real home.

Life Perspectives

Growth

Have you ever heard how Chinese bamboo grows? This tree when planted, watered, and nurtured for an entire growing season doesn't seem to have grown as much as an inch. Then, after the second growing season, a season in which the farmer takes extra care to water, fertilize and care for the bamboo tree, the tree still hasn't shown any signs of growth. So it goes for four straight years. The farmer has very little to show for all his efforts.

Then, along comes year five. That Chinese bamboo tree finally comes forth and then grows up to eighty feet in just one growing season!

Did the little tree lie dormant for four years only to grow exponentially in the fifth? No—during those four years it was developing a massive root system strong enough to support its potential for outward growth.

Our lives are like that. Sometimes it feels like we're studying and practicing and remembering and putting our focus on feeling our hearts and opening our minds and living in expanded awareness—yet it hardly seems like anything is happening. And then all of a sudden, it feels as if our whole lives have moved to a whole new level.

So today, just take time to nurture that which is real. Take time to nurture thoughts that are kind and loving about yourself and about your world. What you'll notice over time is you'll look back and you'll say, "This is a whole new life, how did this happen?" Well, it happened a little at a time—and all at once.

Self-Talk

Scientists say that 92 percent of the time we are talking to ourselves. If we pay attention, there is a lot of internal dialogue that we're engaging in almost all the time.

What is the general tone of that dialogue? Are your thoughts simply the patterns that you inherited, repeating over and over, or are you truly using your creative capacity to engineer thoughts that will yield the result you want most?

Emerson said, "Stand guard at the portal of your mind."

Make your thoughts supportive and encouraging. We remind ourselves that there is a Presence and there is a Power that is right with us that is greater than anything we're facing.

So today, let's pay attention to that self-talk and shift it to a higher octave, and speak to ourselves the way we would really hope others would speak to us as well, then notice what happens.

Pulling Our Problems

As I travel, I often take my rolling computer bag, which has a long handle on it so I can avoid having to carry all of the things I need to have while I'm on the plane.

I used to have a habit of pushing the bag in front of me. Any time it hit a bump or anytime a door threshold was there, it would cause a stumble for me. It was actually so much more difficult to push it.

Then I begin to notice that if I would pull the bag instead, I could actually pull it with my little finger. I thought about the law of physics and how much easier it is to pull than to push—and how that works with our own life issues.

When I let my issues lead me, when I let my concerns lead me, any little bump can throw me off. But if I put them behind me like Jesus said, "Get thee behind me," then whatever it is, I am able to handle. The strength that is required to handle whatever shows up can be as little as the power in my little finger.

I'm not sure that's the law of physics, but I'll bet it's a law of metaphysics.

Start at the End

Sometimes the greatest lessons come from children.

I was out to eat with my little granddaughter, Allie. The waiter gave her a small placemat menu with a maze on it.

She smiled and said, "Amma, I want to show you something." She took her finger to the maze and put it right to the end where you're supposed to come out and then traced backwards to the beginning. She then took her pencil and found her way very easily to the end.

She said, "If you start at the end first, then you know where you want to end up, it's easier to find your way."

I said, "You know what Allie, that's just how it is in life. If you know where you want to end up, it's a whole lot easier to find your way."

With this lesson I want you to ask yourself, "Where do I want to end up myself?"

"Where do I really want to be in relationship with the important people in my life, with the earth, with myself, with my creative capacity? Where do I want to end up when I put my head on the pillow the very last time?"

Because when we know where we want to end up, the feelings that we're having, the thoughts that we know; it's a whole lot easier to find our way.

The Squeeze of Life

I remember hearing Wayne Dyer once speak about what happens when an orange is squeezed. He said, "When you squeeze an orange, what comes out of it?" His answer, of course, was orange juice. Then he looked at the audience and said, "Why does orange juice come out of an orange when it's squeezed?" Then he laughed and said, "Because that's what was in there all along."

There is hardly a day that goes by without us getting a little bit of a squeeze from life itself. There may be traffic to deal with or a child who doesn't do what we'd hoped they would or did something we hoped they wouldn't. Or, we ourselves, disappoint ourselves or aren't able to show up in all the ways we wish we could.

As we get squeezed by disappointment or the hurt of a let down or by frustration, what will come out of us is deeply connected to what's going on in our faith practice.

So as you and I recognize that every single experience that happens in our lives can be an experience to take us closer to God, all of a sudden, everything begins to change. Instead of wanting things to change, we recognize that WE can change.

As we begin to embrace the opportunity to appreciate what is, all of a sudden, what is is wonderful!

So today, when you get squeezed a bit by what's going on in your life, make the conscious decision to say, "May I learn from this, may I grow from this."

Open Heart

Have you ever gone to an open house? Maybe it's a real estate open house or an open house hosted by a family. Whatever type of open house it is, you know a lot of preparation has gone into it.

Often there are refreshments, like cookies or something to drink. The place is neat and tidy, the lights are warm and inviting, the doors are open and it's a welcoming experience.

Imagine today creating in your heart an open house for God. An open house to welcome in this day fully.

So the table is set, the drinks are prepared, the cookies have been baked, and the food's been laid out. Inside your heart you are perfectly ready for this day to fully receive the gift, the miracles, the grace of this day.

Oh Well

A long time ago, someone gave me a clue about how to deal with things that can't be changed.

If you had a plate in your hand and then dropped it, watching it shatter, immediately upon seeing its broken pieces you'd know it couldn't be put back together.

Or perhaps you left a little late and now you're stuck in traffic. It's like a parking lot and you're just sitting there, going nowhere.

When you're in situations you know can't be changed, there are two power words that you can speak in that moment and they are simply these, "Oh well." If you can't change it, when you say, "Oh well", then you open up to what CAN be.

Because the parking lot on the freeway can be a Zen monastery, it can be a place where we can say, "Oh well, I can't change the traffic but I can change how I am while sitting in the traffic."

I can't change the broken plate, but I can change how I respond to the broken plate. I can say, "Oh well, the plate is broken. So what can I bring together now in this moment of my life?"

We take the moments today we can't change that we wish we could and we look upon them and we simply say, "Oh well." And we practice being in the Zen monastery of an awakened day which is always a miracle in the making.

Fun

In the early '70s some very powerful research began that has most recently been documented by Harvard and the major medical schools in America, which says that when we have fun, we are healthier.

When we have fun, our brain actually emits different chemicals that send the signals "Live, be well, be alert, be vital," to every cell in our bodies.

Our cells are activated and we move into a whole new stream of aliveness when we have fun. So I would encourage us to say to ourselves, "you know what, I get to choose the experience I'm having today."

That's metaphysics 101. I get to choose the experience I'm having. I'm going to choose today, in the midst of whatever I'm doing, to see the bright side of things, to bring humor and a merry heart to things, which is good like a medicine.

I will take my medicine today, and it shall be fun!

Perspective

When you and I are standing on the ground looking at the conditions of our lives, we see only one perspective. But, if we go up inside a tall building and look at the same scenery, we see a whole different perspective. And, when are in an airplane, we see even more.

You and I can bring a different perspective to whatever condition, whatever situation, whatever dream is present in our lives right now.

Let's practice today not just seeing things from one viewpoint—right up close, how it appears, what the surface looks like; let's go broader, higher, wider—and let's go even deeper and ask each one of those conditions to share its viewpoint with us.

Then we will get a much stronger vision and an even bigger picture. Only then can we truly unwrap the gift that is in the situation we're facing today.

So today we are practicing a wider, broader perspective—seeing with the eyes of God.

Up Until Now

A number of years ago someone gave me a phrase to practice when I wanted to overcome a self-defeating pattern.

We all have patterns of thinking that are less than who we really are. We learned them as kids or we learned them because something happened and we began to believe something about ourselves that produced a limiting experience.

So whenever you have a limiting thought where you think "I can't do that," or "I don't have enough of this," or "it's too late," or "I should have done it sooner," just to say to yourself, "Up until now, that has been true about me."

Those words, "Up Until Now" are a powerful message to the subconscious mind. They are a new order coming in. They are saying that the order that was established in the past is no longer in power, by the authority that is given each one of us, in our freedom of choice, in our free will. We get to choose a new pattern when we say so.

When the old pattern emerges trying to give life to itself one more time, we say to it, "Up until now it might have been true, but not now. Now, this is true." We begin to establish a new pattern of thinking and that new pattern begins to take on a life of itself. That life becomes our life.

So today we say "Up Until Now" to everything that is limiting, and we lay claim to the power of God that is in us to describe and decide the life we would have.

The Glass Is Refillable

It's said that attitude is not only important, attitude is everything. Attitude is the lens through which we perceive and then experience our lives. We don't see life as it is, we see life as we are.

My stepson Matthew is a kid who has conditions that have made traditional learning difficult for him. And, he is a kid who is porous to aliveness and fresh in the green growing edges of his own becoming. He has taught me many things.

One of the lessons he taught me was this—he looked at me and he said,

> *"You know Mom, an optimist says a glass is half full, a pessimist says a glass is half empty, but you know what I say, I say, 'That glass is refillable.'"*

I laughed at the time, but I thought so many times. "If we could only remember, half full/half empty is just an opinion. We choose what our focus is."

The truth is that is there is an ever flow of fresh, living water for our day.

This glass—our life, this moment—is refillable when we remember God.

Do-Overs

There is a term in golf called a mulligan. In human relations the same term is simply a "do-over".

If you ever find yourself saying something that you wish you hadn't said, or wishing you hadn't done what you just did, it is really helpful to look at the other person and simply say, "You know what, I'd like a do-over." Then come from your best self.

So whatever is going on for you today and whoever you're interacting with, including yourself, it is great to know that at any moment you choose, you can say, "I'd like a do-over."

Then just give the best that you have from the insight you've just learned in that situation. It's helpful. It's good. It's feedback from our Higher Self to our conscious mind when we don't feel right about something we did.

Simply ask for a "do-over" and your Best Self will come right through.

Good Morning

You know most of us will say several times a day, "good morning," "good afternoon," or "good evening."

That phrase, good evening, good morning, good afternoon actually began in the middle ages when people were saying, "God in the morning," "God in the evening," "God in the afternoon."

And then somewhere down the line it got turned into a contraction, where we just say "good morning."

We know that God is good, so in a sense, we are really saying, "God in the morning."

But today, just for today, practice every time you hear or say, "Good morning" that what you really feel is God is in this morning. God is in this afternoon. God is in this evening.

Walk this day remembering who walks with you.

The Elephant Story

Four blind men were sharing their ideas about what they thought an elephant was like.

One of the blind men was touching the elephant's tail and said, "The elephant is like a rope." Another touching the elephant's leg said, "No, an elephant is not like a rope, an elephant is like a tree trunk." The one touching the elephant's side belly said, "No, an elephant is not like a rope or a tree trunk, an elephant is like a wall." The other, touching the elephant's trunk said, "No, not like a wall, not like a tree trunk, not like a rope, it's a hose. An elephant is like a big hose."

Every one of these men was accurate in their description according to their own perspective. You and I are, in a sense, blinded to the whole picture of what is at work in our lives right now. We are only touching, if you will, a portion of the activity of the presence of God in our lives.

So we tend to believe a circumstance or a situation means something—and it isn't that we're wrong—it can mean exactly that from our perspective, but there's more. Part of the gift of experiencing miracles is staying aware to the more-ness that we don't know, to stay in the mystery. To know that even if we can't see the miracle, we can trust in it.

Let today be one of a deepening kind of trust that opens your perception to the miracle in the making called YOU!

Alignment

A few weeks ago my car was so out of alignment that it just wouldn't drive properly. It had a big powerful engine. There was plenty of gas in the tank. It had all kinds of things that worked just fine. But, because it was out of alignment the ride was really bumpy and somewhat out of control.

The same thing happens in our lives. Each one of us is a powerful, powerful, spiritual being. When we get out of alignment—get too weighted down with doing and not enough of being; when we get too busy with creating and trying to achieve or acquire and we forget to have quiet moments where we can hear the still, small voice—then the ride gets bumpy and can even get out of control.

So today, let's get into alignment with the gift that something wonderful is happening to us this day, this thing called life.

The most important thing for this day is that we learn to live and give and see love. Nothing can keep us from that when we stay in alignment with what's really important.

Connectedness

I'm writing this from Times Square in downtown New York City.

Amid all the hustle and bustle, I'm reminded that no matter where we are, no matter what is going on, amidst all the different people in our lives and in the world, there is a language that is being spoken—and that is the language of LIFE.

That language is making your heart beat right now, it's breathing you. That language of life is breathing and moving throughout the entire planet and the entire universe.

We are part of something that is magnificent. Pause where you are right now and tune into that and just feel the miracle of your own being—and become aware of this amazing life.

You get to make a miracle today wherever you are, because you're a part of it—if you just remember.

Focus

The other day I was driving past a Ford dealership and noticed a flashing sign that read, "Rent a Focus."

I thought, "Wow, what if we really could rent a focus?" If you could rent a focus, which means to bring a higher quality of paying attention today, what would you ask to have more focus for?

What would you like to see more clearly? What would you like to know more deeply? What would you like to feel more fully?

Today, we really can rent a focus by asking that we see with the eyes that God gave us—which are the eyes of the heart.

Smiling

I have a friend who was telling me recently that our body does not know the difference between a real smile and a fake smile.

What happens when we put a smile on our face is that there are endorphins that are released by the brain that move through the body which raise our immune system, increase our aliveness and open the door to creativity.

Now, if we have an authentic smile that's hooked to our emotional system, then of course there are more endorphins and more response. Nevertheless, as the Seicho-No-Ie group in Japan says,

> *"You can be happy and then laugh,*
> *or you can laugh and be happy.*
> *Both ways work."*

Today, let's put a smile on our face and just trust that the reason God gave us a way to smile is because it's hooked to a system inside of ourselves. That system is wired to what we're really here for, and that is to experience, express and live in the love that is the Source of our life.

So right now, join me and let's put a smile on our face.

The Miracle of Love

Drink Love

It was Hafiz, the poet, who wrote:

> *"I know the way you can get when you have not had a drink of love. Your face hardens. Your sweet muscles cramp. Children become concerned about a strange look that appears in your eyes, which even begins to worry your own mirror and knows. Even angels fear that brand of madness that arrays itself against the world. Oh the way I know that you can get if you have not been out drinking love."*

Our opportunity today, and really our responsibility today, is to drink from Love's Presence. To let It in. To know that we are so loved in the midst of and in the presence of everything that is our life this day.

The poet continues,

> *"This is why all the great ones speak of the vital need to keep remembering God. So you will come to know and see Him as being so playful and wanting, just wanting to help. Bring your cup near me, dear one. Bring your cup near me for all I care about is quenching your thirst for freedom."*

I know the way you can get if you have been out drinking Love. It becomes a miracle! So let this be a day of drinking in the Love.

What Would Love Do?

What if by the end of this week we could look back and say, "This was one of the most wonderful weeks of my life?"

You and I have an opportunity to create such a week by making an intention right now that this week we will stay close to God. We will make our will God's will. Meaning that again and again, we will ask ourselves this question; "What would love do here?"

As we ask that question, stay in that question, listen for guidance and follow that guidance, we catch a current. There is a current of our own life force, which is one with God already, one with love already. As we simply move into that current, we are lifted up.

There is a week that is available to each and every one of us where we will look back and say, "Oh, my God, thank you. Thank you."

Let's lean into the question, "What would love do here?" and be lifted up in love every moment.

Love Affair With Life

I've been reading the poetry of Hafiz, the Persian poet from the 1300's who writes about having a love affair with life itself, right in the midst of our daily living.

I want to share this one sweet little poem from his writings:

> *"We have all come to the right place.*
> *We all sit in God's classroom.*
> *Now, the only thing left for us to do*
> *my dear, is to stop throwing spitballs*
> *for a while."*

Can you imagine how wonderful that thought is? The curriculum is perfect. In a sense we have been throwing spitballs saying, "I want this to be different, change this, fix that," rather than embracing, opening up to, and inviting the curriculum of love to have its way with us this day.

Every single thing in our life is patterned for our growth, for our becoming, to support us in experiencing the power and the wonder and the gift of our aliveness.

So let's tune into our day with a great gratitude—and have a love affair with Life!

Small Things With Great Love

Mother Teresa said,

> *"We can do no great things; we can do only small things with great love."*

We can do no great things; we can do small things with great Love.

So what if we took what that small woman practiced, which absolutely transformed the thinking of millions and millions of people on this planet and employed it in our lives today? What if today was about each one of us showing up as a representation, as a representative of the One who gives us life?

"For this we came into the world, to give witness to the glory of the One who indwells us"—and that One is God whose name is Love.

Today, let us go into everything we're doing, every conversation we have, not seeking to do great things but doing small things with great love. Great Love.

What if great Love showed up today in your family and you were the avenue through which it did? What if great Love showed up today in all the places you went because you accessed that great Love who has called you into life, who gave you birth, who's breathing you right now?

We can do no great things, but we can do small things with great Love.

Shower the People

I woke up this morning, and in my early meditation
I heard these words from the James Taylor song,

> *"Shower the people you love with love. Show them the way you feel. Things are going to work out a whole lot better if you will."*

So as we move through our day with all our "to do" lists and all of the things that are required to get us through our day, we can lose sight of what is most important.

But if we remember Jesus' words that the most important thing in life is love—to love God, to love each other—we will shower the people (that includes yourself) who are closest to us with love. We will shower everyone we encounter today with love.

Shower the people you love with love. Show them the way you feel. Things are going to work out a whole lot better if you will.

Harnessing the Energies of Love

The great philosopher Teilhard de Chardin said,

> *"Once man has mastered the winds and the waves, gravity and the sky; he shall harness for God the energies of love and then for the second time in the history of the world, man will have discovered fire."*

Well, with technology we have mastered a whole lot—certainly the winds and the waves in some regard. We haven't learned to control nature, but we have learned how to work with nature in many ways. Have we outstripped our technology in that direction compared to how well we have learned to harness the energies of Love?

Imagine harnessing the energies of Love. What might that mean to ourselves, to our families, to our workplace and to our world? Many of us would like someone else to figure out how to master and harness the energies of Love, but who is going to be the one to do it? It is going to be you and it's going to be me.

So today, let each of us focus on how we could harness the energies of Love for ourselves, for our families, for our workplace, and ultimately for a better world.

Love Made Visible

Let's pause for a moment and consider the idea of our work as a sacrament.

It was Khalil Gibran who said,

> *"True work is love made visible."*

Love made visible. Now whether our work is cutting hair, delivering mail, working as an executive, managing a household, changing diapers, doing laundry, cooking, washing dishes; whatever the work is, it is equally opportunistic to be a sacrament of holy activity.

Every one of us has some work to do today to not only help ourselves and our families, but our world become the expression of the Divine that is within us.

It isn't the thing we're doing; it is how we're doing the thing we're doing. Mother Theresa said, "It is not that we're to do great things but we're to do the things we do with great love."

So true work then is love made visible. Let's you and I bring the holy of holies right to what we're doing this day and recognize that as we know this, everything, everything is Holy Now.

Fall In Love

Matthew Fox was a Catholic priest who "woke up" and began teaching beyond the boundaries of the training he'd been given. He was at first silenced, and then eventually kicked out of the Catholic church for his teachings.

After he had been silenced for a year, I happened to have the honor of being in the audience when he gave his first talk.

He got up, looked around the room, stood in silence for a moment and then he said, "And as I was saying." He then went on giving the message he had always been giving. That message is that there is this Universal Christ Presence that indwells every one of us. It is our potential and it is our purpose.

One of the ways he says to access our potential and purpose is to fall in love at least three times a day. At least three times a day, just fall in love with your life or an expression of it. Fall in love with a bird you hear singing or a cat you see curled up or with a dog licking a child's face. Fall in love with life in all its many dimensions and all the ways it presents itself to you, at least three times a day.

So today, we make a choice right now. This day I shall fall in love with life at least three times.

Life Moments

Look Around

I was with a friend who was taking me to the airport and we stopped to get a bite to eat. Next door to the place we were sitting was a market that had the most beautiful array of flowers.

I paused for a moment and just took it all in. I said to her, "Look at those flowers, they're just offering themselves to this day!" My friend smiled and said, "Wow, thank you for that moment."

I realized how often it is that we can offer each other moments that help us go deeper. But, more than that, when someone offers us a moment, if we acknowledge it, it amplifies the moment for everyone.

So today, pay attention to moments; special recognitions of the Power of God and the gift of Life that you can offer those you are around.

When you feel a moment offered to you, celebrate not only the Power that gives you the moment, but the one who reminded you it was there.

What Matters Most

Last night I was sitting with my two-year-old grandson, Joel. I had given him a tiny little chalkboard with a little box of chalk in which there perhaps half a dozen pieces. When he opened the box and pulled out the chalk, two of the pieces broke and then as he played with them a few more pieces broke off.

When it was time to put them away, he attempted to put the chalk back in the box. He put the little pieces in first and then the big pieces wouldn't fit. So I was showing him that if he would put the big pieces in first, then the little pieces could fit around those big pieces and he could get everything into the box.

I was reminded of how that is with our lives. If we let our lives get filled up with the unimportant—with the many phone calls or emails or things that come our way without knowing what the big pieces are, what really matters to us—our life gets filled up with a whole lot of little things and eventually what was really important to us doesn't fit anymore.

So today would be a great day to pause and ask, "Deep down inside of me, what really matters? What are the one or two or three things that I want to be sure gets fit into the core and center of my life?

From this, emerges a whole new kind of life and that truly is a miracle.

Water Energy

I write this as I am sitting next to a waterfall at the hotel where I stayed last night. I am thinking about how scientists tell us that falling waters and large bodies of water produce something called negative ions which create the conditions that make it easier for us to have clarity of thinking.

Often some of our best ideas can happen near places of water—like in the shower.

So today, as you splash water on your face to wash it, or drink a glass of water, or anytime you wash your hands, just open up to the possibility that in that moment there may be a great thought trying to come your way. Remember, God's currency is in ideas.

So know this: Everything you're looking for is available to you today in the energy of water. God is all around you and within you. Pay attention and you may find your best thoughts are in some falling water.

The Perfect Day

Imagine that right now someone is saying to you, "I lovingly and gently invite you to join me in creating a perfect day." I gently and lovingly invite you to join me in creating a Perfect Day.

Imagine now that the Voice you hear is the voice of God—that your day begins right now as you hear these words.

From this moment forward, feel how it feels to be in a co-creative process with the One who gives you life. It is your opportunity and your right to create a perfect day, which means that everything that happens has a miracle inside of it.

Every word that's spoken has a gift for you. Every bird that you hear, every weed that you see, everything has a gift of aliveness and this message: "Right where you are, God is."

So, here we go, let's create a perfect day.

The Great Adventure

I'm on plane headed off to Big Sky, Montana for a week-long retreat. You know, whenever I get on a plane or I'm getting into a car to travel someplace, I always think, "We're just beginning an adventure!"

Sitting here I had this thought, "You know, we're all traveling." This planet is twirling through space. The universe itself is moving and evolving. Even when we think we're standing still, the fact is, we are part of this evolving, moving, changing universe. If we could just remember that, every single day could be approached as an adventure.

You have never lived this day before. There are things that will happen this day. People that will show up in your life. Approach everything that happens with a curiosity and a wonder.

So I want to invite you into the great adventure that is called your life. It is a miracle to be unwrapped!

The Right Spot

Have you ever noticed that during events like the Academy Awards or a major movie premier, the commentators and news people will say, "Oh, she was so beautiful." Or, "Didn't he look handsome?" Those may be accurate statements about external things.

Have you ever noticed, though, whenever someone is really in their right spot—like a mother holding her baby, or someone lovingly cooking a meal, or someone playing ball with their son, or just moments when we are really in our right spot; if we're paying attention, what might rise up in us is, "Isn't that beautiful? Aren't they beautiful?" because there is a radiance to that kind of beauty that comes with being in our right spot.

So today, as you go through your day, let's pay attention to what we really feel—all the way through with all the many parts of ourselves—right with the spot we're in, with the role we're playing, the acts we're doing, with the love we're giving.

There will be a radiance, which is the love and the beauty of God. That beauty is our job, our opportunity, and our gift to bring to the world today. The right spot.

The Gift of Music

Have you ever thought about how every single piece of music is really just vibrations? That's what sound is.

Have you also thought about how your own body resonates with music? It re-sounds.

There is a vibration that happens in us that is our own very aliveness when music and smell and fragrance touches us.

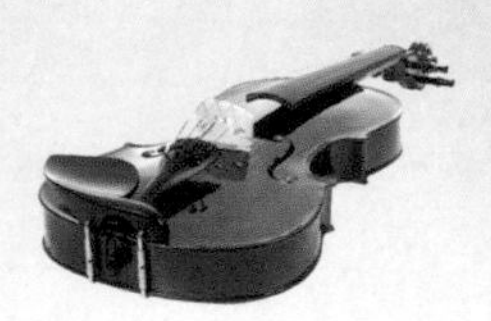

So today, let's pick at least one piece of music that feels good to us, and listen to it. Because our body really can read that sound and it actually affects us at a cellular level. It actually increases our immune system and we become different in the presence of all music.

It doesn't have to be great music, it only has to be music that seems great to you.

What makes it great music? It's great to you—whatever is great to you. Listen to a piece of music. Do it as soon as you can and notice how your day is different.

Call It

There were three umpires talking and one of them said, "Well, I calls them as I sees them." The next one says, "I calls them as they is." And the third one says, "I know this, they ain't nothing 'til I calls them."

So it is with every moment. It isn't good and it isn't bad, it really is neutral. It's nothing 'til we call it.

Today there will be moments that will happen in your life that will never, ever happen again, not ever. Today is a unique, unrepeatable, miracle day.

So today, I invite every one of us to make these moments matter. To hold this day as the precious gift it is and to realize, "I have the opportunity! There will be moment after moment today, and I get to call every single moment what I choose!"

Today we can make every single moment matter as we hold gratitude for the preciousness of our lives.

In God We Trust

As I was sitting in the park, I noticed a penny, a shiny penny underneath the bench. And on this shiny little penny, I read the words, "In God we trust."

You know, even the smallest bit of trust, what seems like just a seed—if you have trust and faith even the size of a mustard seed, then you can do great things.

So right now you have trust, you have faith—all that is required. To everyone is given this measure of faith. Nobody in the world has more faith than you or me. It is just a matter of what we are interested in, because that is where we are putting our faith.

So let's be interested in that which is life-giving, be interested in that which is contributory and be interested in how we might be of service. Be interested this day in appreciating the love that is in our lives.

In God we trust. In God we have faith. It is not only on a penny; it is a way to live a life in abundance.

Pet Friends

Many of us have had a pet in our lives.

Imagine that pets are God's idea for teaching us another kind of love that we would never know from our human encounters.

Wherever you are today, whether it is the birds singing outside our windows, the affection from our dogs or our cats, or the squirrels outside our window—whatever kind of wildlife or nature is around you; today just open up to the idea that every one of the animals on this Earth have a message to teach us about love.

May we want to know and learn the unique way these creatures are presenced on this earth by a Creator who loves us and is wise beyond our understanding in all the ways that the curriculum of love might be delivered to us. There is much to learn in the love and joy our pets bring to us.

So may we be a good student this day of all the ways we're being instructed to love through our animal friends.

The "Wow" Factor

I was driving to the airport with my husband, Joe. I don't remember exactly what had happened, but Joe said, "Wow." Then he looked at me and said, "You know, enough 'Wow' moments add up to a really 'Wow' day, and enough 'Wow' days add up to a really 'Wow' life." Then we began to talk about how you can notice the "Wow."

Certainly there are things that just "Wow" us on their own and other times we find that if we just pay attention to the wonder, to the gift, to the specialness of life, then we see that it's a "Wow" moment all the time with life unfolding itself to us.

I was out last night picking some cherry tomatoes from an abundant cherry tomato plant so we could bring some of those home-grown tomatoes with us for our trip today. I remember looking at that plant going "Wow, look at how nature does this. Look at these beautiful tomatoes."

I don't know what's in your life today, but I know this—if you choose to pay attention to the "Wow," by the time you put your head on the pillow tonight; you will have had a "Wow" day!

I Have All Day

Have you ever been in line someplace and heard somebody in front of you who's waited a long time say to the clerk, "You know, I don't have all day."

Have you ever said that yourself? "I don't have all day."

Let's pause for a moment and realize—you know what, we *do* have all day. We have been given a precious gift. It's all day, one whole day to choose to feel and share and care and love and give and receive and experience the precious, precious gift of this life.

So today, just stop for a moment, and go, "Wow, I do have ALL day and I get to choose."

God's Gift in Leftovers

I did a little poll with the people I was with this morning about leftovers. It was interesting that some of the people thought the leftovers were better than the main meal, while others didn't really care to eat the leftovers.

It just reminded me how everything is neutral until we charge it with our opinions.

What if we looked at what looks like leftovers in our lives—the small tasks, menial things, things that we really haven't looked at as an opportunity to embrace the gift of God?

So, I invite you today to pay attention to all the things in your life that look like leftovers and ask God to show you the gift of the moment. Have fun, by the way!

Coincidence

I was speaking one February at a church in the Pacific Northwest, and between the two services I stepped out back. Just to my left was a plant that was blooming right there in the cold. It appeared to be a daphne plant. I smelled the little flower and just appreciated the effort of its blooming even in the winter.

Then as I attempted to go back inside, I noticed that door had locked. So I went to the next door, which stepped me right inside the bookstore.

As I looked to the left, I saw a book by Howard Thurman. I love his writing. He is an African American mystic who taught at Morehouse College, who mentored Martin Luther King, Jr. and I saw a book title that I had never known he'd written. So I wondered if perhaps I was supposed to buy this book.

I casually opened the book and read the first paragraph my eye fell on and it said, "There is a daphne plant outside my window. The daphne needs struggle in order for its rooting to get really strong so it can bloom fully."

I realized here in a moment I had seen a daphne plant and was led to a book and given a message. It was Carl Jung who said, "Coincidence is God's way of wishing to remain anonymous."

So I invite you this day to look for the coincidence. God remaining anonymous but fully present in your life.

Flexibility

It is very, very windy where I am today As I took a moment to look at swaying trees, I was noticing that some of the trees had fallen down in the wind, while other trees seemed to do really well even in high winds because they have flexibility.

They have evolved themselves to a place where even in high winds they can move with the current conditions in such a way that the wind moves through them rather than pushing against them.

So whatever the winds are doing in your life right now, practice being flexible to the condition that you're in and invite it to offer its gift to you.

Having been through some high winds in my own life, I know that there is a part of us we can find that is flexible enough for anything! Oh my, God is good all the time, even when I struggle to find it.

Rising Above

Float Above It

Eleanor Roosevelt is a woman who has been one of my personal heroes. A woman who took a stand for showing up in fullness at a time when many women were considered to be background people and weren't supposed take a full stand in positions.

She had some important things to say in regard to how to do that. I want to offer you one of her great comments. She said,

> *"All the water in the world cannot drown you unless it gets inside of you."*

So no matter what the problem or difficulty or history or financial situation is in your life, let it be around you. It's a circumstance. It's around you. It is not meant to control or determine your internal weather.

Our internal weather comes from the state of mind and the state of our heart. So we keep our mind and our heart focused on gratitude and appreciation knowing that all the water in the world can be around us, but that we can float on top of it.

In fact, what we find is the ocean delights to lift us as we let go; it lifts us up. So we let go today. We let God and we have a great day.

Your Big God

When we think of the story of David and Goliath, there are some important points to remember.

David knew better than to try to tackle the giant in giant's garb. He shrugged off the heavy armor that was offered him and reached instead for tools that were natural to him. He chose five smooth stones from a riverbed and he put them in a bag with his sling.

David said to Goliath, "You come at me with a sword and a spear and a javelin but I come to you in the name of a Higher Power." That Higher Power is named I Am and that I Am is what's in every one of us.

Armed with the tools that he knew to be his strength and with God, he threw a stone at the giant and the giant fell. David knew that no matter how small he appeared, his faith was bigger than that goliath soldier.

I don't know what your goliath might be right now but I know that if you draw upon resources that are natural to you—which is who You really are, you are a son or a daughter of the most high—you will harness the Divine strength you need to overcome, no matter what.

Instead of telling God about your big goliath, tell your goliath about your big God. Every morning spend just a few minutes filling your mind so full of God that there's no room left for worry.

The Miracle of Enthusiasm

Today let us be in the miracle of what it means to generate enthusiasm.

Enthusiasm is a stream of power that is available to every one of us when we simply choose to allow ourselves to be enthusiastic about whatever we're doing.

Henry Truman said,

> *"I've studied the lives of great men and famous women and I have found that the men and women who got to the top in their field and who were able to say they felt their lives to be a success were simply those who did the jobs they had at hand with every thing they had of energy and enthusiasm."*

Enthusiasm is something we can generate; entheos—God within, God in hand, God right here, God right now in the job that is at hand.

Today let us experience from a decision point the miracle of great enthusiasm.

Spiritual Solutions

Most of us will never forget where we were on September 11, 2001, the day of the most dramatic attack on U.S. soil that's ever happened in the history of the United States.

Well, on that same day in *USA Today*, the newspaper that's circulated to every single city in the United States and all around the world, there was a full-page ad for Wayne Dyer's new book that year whose title read, "There is a Spiritual Solution to Every Problem."

I've always felt that it was no accident that on the day our attention was grabbed by terror, we were also presented with a full-page ad that said there's a spiritual solution to every problem we have.

So, as we take inventory of what's happened in our lives since that event, what have the years brought for us? Have we become more spiritually minded in how we approach our daily life? Are we still fighting an enemy out there? Or, as Mother Teresa said when she was asked why she did what she did, she said, "It's both by the love of my lord, Jesus, that in every person I meet I see his face and also my fear of the little Hitler that resides in the corners of my own heart."

Every one of us has a minor terrorist in ourselves and at the same time there is a great Love that resides in us that can lift us up and lead us to the spiritual solution that not only helps us but our world.

Today, may we each be the solution we're wanting to find in our world.

Lift Your Vision

In the Old Testament we read,

> *"I will lift up mine eyes to the hills from whence cometh my strength."*

I will lift up my eyes to the hills. So right now let's do that, just lift your eyes upwards a bit, close your eyes, your outside eyes and open your inside eyes.

Lift your eyes upward right to the middle of your forehead. There is a place in the middle of your forehead, actually there is a gland there called the pineal gland. When you focus on that part of your body, there's actually energy that moves in and to you—it can move through your thinking and your feeling and change everything for your day.

I will lift up mine eyes to the hills from whence cometh my strength. The strength of inspiration, the strength of wisdom, the strength of healing, the strength of transformation.

Does It Really Matter?

Someone shared a story with me about a friend of theirs who would occasionally say something that really helped put things into perspective.

He'd hit a bad golf shot or he'd get stuck in traffic, even during the big things that happened in life he would say,

> *"In the light of eternity, how can this possibly make any difference?"*

In the light of eternity, how can this possibly make any difference?

So today as we go through the normal things that happen in life, let's keep an eternal perspective that each one of us is here to bear witness to the glory of the One who indwells us.

In light of eternity, all the little things that happen, how can they possibly make any difference? The difference is how we handle the things that really don't matter and bring in the things that really do.

So in the light of eternity, you bringing forth your light does make a difference. In the light of eternity, you discovering who you really are does make a difference. Let's keep that eternal perspective.

Making Weather

Did you know you can create your own weather?

Before we become spiritually aware, we believe that the outside weather has to change before our inside weather can change.

Over time, as we wake up, we realize that our life is determined by our internal weather, not the external weather.

So if you want sunshine today or if you want to be in the dark inside a big storm, you get to be whatever you want by what you focus on internally.

If you want to have a day in which the sun is shining brightly and you're able to see all of the beauty and the glory and the wonder that is around you, start from within. No matter what the outside is doing, even when it's raining, it can be absolutely gorgeous if the internal weather is set for good. I am at one today with my internal weather of choice.

Make the choice and then see what happens.

The Magic Word

Earl Nightingale, years ago created a program called, The Magic Word.

The whole program was designed to help you discover what the magic word was. When you discovered what the magic word was, then you had power.

What you finally discovered through his program was that the magic word was "attitude." When you finally understood the power of your attitude, you understood the power you could wield.

There is a wonderful saying that says,

> *"Attitude is your paintbrush. It colors the way you see things."*

So today let's each recognize that we hold the magic word and it really is the authority and power with which we see things and the way in which we create our lives. That magic is our attitude. Let us choose carefully for in that is the power of the day.

Pause Power

There are defining moments in every one of our lives and those defining moments happen at the moment we decide what something means. Because as soon as we decide what it means, it then becomes true for us.

Every one of us will experience something in our lives that will tempt us to say, "There is nothing good in this experience."

I want to introduce you to a very powerful practice called Pause Power. No matter what you're facing, no matter what happens, no matter what occurs when you are tempted to believe, "ooh this is really bad," stop for a moment and just enter into the power of this practice.

Say to yourself "I am going to wait three days and my only question will be 'Life, show me how to use this—instead of as a stumbling block—as a stepping stone.'" In Scripture it says "all things can work together for good for those who love God." All things, not just some things, all things, even this.

So we say "God, Life, the Presence and Power that guides this Universe, show me how to use this very thing that on the surface looks like something I would never want to have happen in my life. But deep down all things can work together for the good for those who love God.

I turn now to that Infinite support, that Higher Power for guidance in how to turn this into something that not only can be good, but is good.

Earn Your Way Forward

I read an article once on Tiger Woods that really inspired me.

On the way to winning a U.S. Open, Tiger had a healthy lead of a couple of strokes and then on the 14th hole he bogeyed and he only had a one stroke lead. The hottest contender from behind was hitting birdie after birdie after birdie, and moving up ahead.

There came a critical moment in the game where Tiger was going to win or lose the entire match by a putt he needed to make. Later he told the reporters—after his win—that in that moment, what he said to himself was,

> *"Okay, you got yourself into this mess; now earn your way out."*

I thought what a powerful thing for us to consider that we can earn our way into a greater consciousness. We can *earn* our way into a higher performance. We can earn our way into a deeper love.

We make a decision and recognize if we have the power to get ourselves in something, we surely have the power to change things around.

Grit

There is a new movement in America called positive psychology.

A research student discovered something that is very important, the non-IQ predictors of high achievement.

One of those non-IQ predictors of high achievement is called grit. Grit is simply this, how persevering we are in the face of obstacles.

Now if you have an intention for your day, I can promise you this—there will be some obstacles. Those obstacles are not there to stop you, they are there to instruct you about how powerful you really are.

As you surmount those obstacles by touching a part of yourself that is bigger than that obstacle, you discover that there is a power within you greater than anything in the world—and that is spiritual practice my friend.

So, may you have more grit today than you've ever known you had!

Mementos

When Abraham Lincoln was assassinated there were five things that were in his pocket that have been held for all these years at the Smithsonian Institute. When you see the display, it's striking.

There was a confederate coin that he carried. There was handkerchief that was monogrammed with the initials A. L. There was a pocket knife that he had from the time he was a little boy. There was a memento of his mother.

There was also a newspaper article that had been folded and opened and read and re-read many, many times. It was an article written and published in the London Herald by a British news writer who spoke of Abraham Lincoln's leadership during the Civil War. It spoke of how it took such courage and such character that few men could withstand to lead a country during a time of such discontinuity between the North and the South.

The writings that tell why Abraham Lincoln carried that in his pocket said that he faced such great doubt and criticism, that he wondered if he had what it would take to lead the country to what he was called to do. So he kept something in front of him from someone who believed in him even at times when he would forget for himself.

So what is in your pocket today? Put something in your pocket, a scripture or a picture of someone who believes in you—something to remind you that there is a part of you that is bigger and more powerful than you know. That part of you is available to you right now.

Greatness

Reverend Michael Beckwith said something very powerful a few weeks ago,

> *"Mediocrity always attacks excellence."*

We have in us parts that are of genius. A part of us that is really of the One Presence and the One Power. But, we have also been trained to think in ways that actually attack the part of us that is great.

Let us practice being our own very best friends. When we notice attack thoughts coming our way, just say to ourselves, "What is really true about me? I didn't create myself. The One who is the One that is the Spirit of this life created me and has great things to do through me."

So, today I say, let me be an instrument of that greatness. Let's focus our day and release ourselves unto the power of what's possible this day.

Letting Go

There is a spiritual practice called the "Pity Party."

The Pity Party is one of the ways we move negative emotions so that we can free our minds and our hearts to live in the fullness of the present moment. If there's something that you've been bothered about, something that you're upset about or hurt about or disappointed about and it keeps surfacing, throw yourself a Pity Party.

You can even make a cake and invite some friends over if you want. But, make sure it isn't longer than an hour or two. You set a beginning and you set an end and you say, "This is the moment when I'm going to let myself feel sorry for myself and hash over all these negative emotions and then, once and for all, be done with it."

The next time your mind tries to pick that problem up again, you say, "No—I'm taking the lesson from that—I am walking on. I am free. It is in my past. I am brand new here and now."

If you have something that's been bothering you for a long time, throw yourself a little pity party and set yourself free to let go and let God and create a whole new beginning.

A Different World

Non-violence is not "not violence," it is actually another whole order of being.

Mahatma Gandhi's grandson speaks about "satyagraha," which is the practice of a way of being that puts us in touch with a power, "ahimsa," soul force that is greater than anything in this world.

You have a power in you that is greater than discrimination, that is greater than racism, that is greater than poverty, that is greater than all the lack and limited thinking. That power has to move into the world in the place it can—and that is through you and me.

As you and I address our own poverty thinking, as we address our own inner violence where we criticize ourselves and others, as we begin to work with what we call passive violence; we begin to mitigate and diminish the world of outer violence.

So as we notice the news this week, we wish so much that our world would be different. You and I can make a significant difference when we have a criticism-free day for ourselves and each other.

Look for the good and let it flow more fully right where we are.

Take No Offense

Eleanor Roosevelt once said,

> *"You cause as much pain by taking offense as by giving offense."*

You cause as much pain by taking offense as by giving offense.

So today, let us see if we can have one offense-free day where the internal critic—for ourselves or others—is just given the day off. Every time that voice tries to speak we say, "no, you have a day off. I will replace you with a blessing instead."

In 1 Corinthians 13, Paul writes about what love is and what love isn't. One of the things he says about love is that it is never quick to take offense.

So today we turn our offense-taking down. We turn our grace giving up. We just appreciate the opportunity we have to experience life as it is—which includes all of us in our human condition and all of the things that are happening.

We practice bringing grace where we are by taking no offense.

Meet the Author

International Speaker, Best-Selling Author, CEO Consultant, Visionary, Empowerment Specialist

Speaker, best-selling author, and consultant for over three decades, Mary Morrissey's transformational talks and seminars have made her one of the elite teachers in the human potential movement. She is the president and founder of LifeSOULutions, an international company providing programs and products that transform dreams into reality. Her work takes her weekly to different parts of the globe.

Mary is the Co-Founder and the first President of the Association for Global New Thought. Along with Dr. Michael Beckwith, she became the first New Thought minister to be appointed to the Executive Counsel of the Parliament of World Religions. She has served three times at the United Nations as the national Co-Chair for A Season of Non-Violence, and has received the honor of being inducted into the Martin Luther King Order of Preachers.

Mary has spoken at the United Nations, met with Nelson Mandela, co-convened meetings with the Dalai Lama, and authored two best-selling books, *No Less Than Greatness* and *Building Your Field of Dreams.*

As a highly sought after inspirational speaker, executive coach, and ministry consultant, Mary has 30 years of experience empowering individuals in achieving new heights of spiritual aliveness and authentic success.

While she holds significant academic degrees, Mary says her two most important achievements are the two black belts she holds: one in success, and the other in failure.

A complimentary gift for you

Congratulations on finishing *The Miracle Minute* book!

If you want the inspiration to continue, Mary Morrissey has a very special gift waiting just for you.

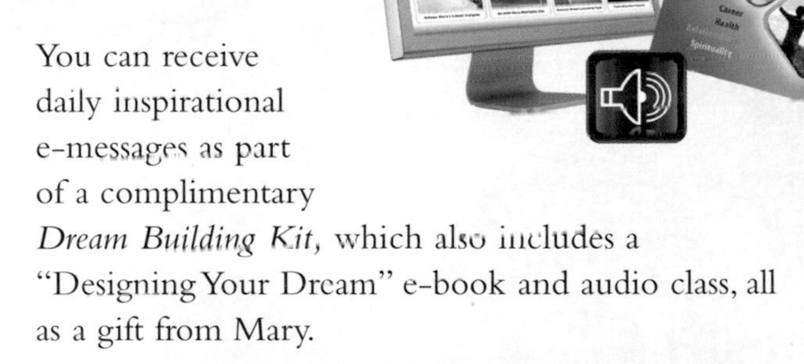

You can receive daily inspirational e-messages as part of a complimentary *Dream Building Kit,* which also includes a "Designing Your Dream" e-book and audio class, all as a gift from Mary.

To receive your complimentary *Dream Building Kit* and continue the inspiration simply go to:

www.MaryMorrissey.com